The House of Hope and Fear

The House of Hope and Fear

Life in a Big City Hospital

Audrey Young, MD

SASQUATCH BOOKS
SEATTLE

Printed in the United States of America
Published by Sasquatch Books
Distributed by PGW/Perseus
15 14 13 12 11 10 09   9 8 7 6 5 4 3 2 1

Cover photograph: 57440217 Stockbyte / Getty Images
Cover design: Judith Stagnitto Abbate / Abbate Design
Interior design and composition: Rosebud Eustace

Marv Hooley's story appeared previously in modified form in "The Hospitalist's
Story," *JAMA*, November 1, 2006; volume 296, page 2067–68, copyright © 2006,
American Medical Association. All rights reserved. Reprinted with permission.

Library of Congress Cataloging-in-Publication Data
Young, Audrey, M.D.
  The house of hope and fear : life in a big city hospital / Audrey Young.
    p. ; cm.
  ISBN-13: 978-1-57061-511-5
  ISBN-10: 1-57061-511-X
  1. Young, Audrey, M.D. 2. Harborview Medical Center (Seattle, Wash.) 3.
Women physicians—Washington (State)—Seattle—Biography. 4. Hospital care—
Washington (State)—Seattle. 5. County hospitals—Washington (State)—Seattle.
I. Title.
  [DNLM: 1. Young, Audrey, M.D. 2. Harborview Medical Center (Seattle,
Wash.) 3. Hospitals, County—Washington—Personal Narratives. 4. Health
Services Accessibility—Washington—Personal Narratives. 5. Physicians, Women—
Washington—Personal Narratives. WX 28 AW2 Y68h 2009]
  R154.Y59A3 2009
  610.92—dc22
  [B]
                            2007013054

Sasquatch Books
119 South Main Street, Suite 400
Seattle, WA 98104
(206) 467-4300
www.sasquatchbooks.com
custserv@sasquatchbooks.com

Author's Note

Doctors refine their craft by talking about their cases and stories with one another. I've tried to write this book in that tradition. To protect privacy, names and identifying details of all patients were altered and in some cases blended to portray common clinical situations. Whenever possible, I obtained permission to use stories from the patients or surviving family members. My own experiences are true, as are those of my colleagues, who appear here under their real names.

Contents

Preface:
A Place for the Poor

The King County hospital opened for business in 1931, near the intersection of Ninth Avenue and Jefferson Street, on a hill above downtown Seattle. The hospital would serve the city's poor and indigent in a stately new $2.75 million facility that featured wide hallways, high ceilings, and sweeping views of the harbor. The building was done in art deco style, according to the latest fashion of the East Coast teaching hospitals, and was a significant upgrade from prior quarters. City newspapers howled over the "exorbitant" cost and political cartoons depicted doctors pouring champagne into the mouths of patients. It was an early rendition on the idea that we should help the poor, but perhaps without spending too much money.

The new county hospital suffered immediately from crowded conditions. A south-facing extension was added some years later, and after the University of Washington medical school assumed management in the 1960s, the complex came to include a north wing, a mental health building, and an upgraded research tower with faculty offices. A west wing with matching yellow brick siding was built in the 1990s, and the hospital at present has eight floors of wards, seven distinct ICUs, sixteen operating suites, and more than 100,000 square feet of clinic space. When viewed from the Seattle harbor, the hospital—now known as Harborview—is an elegant collection of architecturally cohesive structures sitting high atop the city skyline. The place is so large that when a senior medicine resident is at a patient's bedside in the medical ICU on the second floor of the new wing, and there is a Code Blue in the burn ICU on the top floor of the old building, the resident has a one-fifth-mile dash with 130 feet of elevation gain ahead of her.

Despite the vast space, crowds at Harborview still hit capacity on a more or less daily basis, thanks to the wildly expanding pool of the gainfully employed who no longer have health insurance or never had it, and those known in the health services trade as the "underinsured." Some of the hospital's clientele are visible in the immediate neighborhood, emerging from shelters with their life possessions, and queuing up in soup kitchen lines. Others live in the enormous public apartment towers or Section 8 townhouses favored by Somali, Eritrean, and Hmong refugees, many of whom grow radiant flowers and vegetables on their tiny plots of land. Some ride to the hospital from nearby neighborhoods on the numbers 3, 4, and 60 public buses, and some are brought by taxi, squad car, jail van, private vehicle, or ambulance. Those in the greatest hurry come by the airlift helicopter that banks low across Interstate-5 and touches down on the helipad with burn and trauma victims from across the state, and sometimes from as far afield as Alaska, Montana, and northern Idaho.

Because of the hospital's rapidly growing client base, patients who require hospitalization must sometimes wait in the hallways for as long as a day before a legitimate bed becomes available upstairs. The Garden View area, so named by the emergency department staff, was for a time one typical holding space. The view was not of gardens, naturally, but of ambulances unloading patients on the ramp outside. When this temporary unit was pressed into operation, a nurse, cardiac monitoring equipment, oxygen tanks, and ten thinly padded stretchers had to be imported from other locations in the hospital, and makeshift folding curtains were placed between beds for a suggestion of privacy. With the exception of a computer terminal rolled in on a portable desk, Garden View looked like a scene from a period movie.

And so the torrid pace of construction continues. The aging mental health building was recently demolished and foundation poured for a glassy nine-story building that will hold fifty more hospital beds, eight new operating rooms, and several floors of clinics. An entire city block catty-corner from the 1931 building has been leveled to make room for still more medical facilities, displacing a decades-old apartment building, a two-story walk-up, a grocery, a Chinese take-out joint, a dry cleaning business, and convenient parking for families of ICU patients. This city block–size structure will feature retail shops at street level and original artwork in the lobbies, along with many hundreds of thousands of square feet of additional clinic and office space.

If it is impossible to imagine how patients will actually fill the planned space, consider that the same was said a few years earlier about the expanded emergency room and intensive care units, and then about the brand-new observation unit, which was carved from a storage area. Those beds all filled within hours of opening.

Public hospitals originated from eighteenth-century urban almshouses built and run by the wealthy elite, and well-connected physicians were invited into these houses to provide free care for the destitute sick. In time, hospitals developed new medical and surgical therapies that began to draw paying patients, and hospital trustees learned that care for the poor could be funded with the medical fees the better-off patients paid. This commercial transformation continued in the twentieth century, as a new class of hospitals began to offer private rooms with personal steam baths and sunlamps, in hopes of attracting wealthy clients, and abandoned the original charitable function of hospitals. The sick indigent were left for the public hospitals.

Public hospitals came to rely heavily on government funding and volunteer physicians in order to survive, and many became known for overcrowding and squalid conditions, inept management, and inadequate medical care. The private sector maneuvered skillfully to protect its market share, and for a time the California supreme court even held that public hospitals could *only* accept nonpaying patients. Needless to say, many public hospitals did not survive this environment. Among hospitals that closed toward the latter part of the twentieth century was Philadelphia General, the first hospital to open in America, in 1751. Despite these unfavorable circumstances, the King County hospital in Seattle managed to survive.

When I arrived at Harborview for the first time in 1996 as a third-year medical student on the trauma surgery service, I knew next to nothing about the intense pressures facing contemporary public hospitals. To me then, the hospital had only the thumping pulse and plotlessness of a music video. But I was drawn to the energy of the place, and I returned for clinical experiences whenever the opportunity presented itself. Only later would I learn that while I was undergoing my clinical training, between the years 1996 and 2002, one-sixth of the urban public hospitals in the United States shut their doors for good, and in smaller or more remote locales, public hospital closures exceeded one in four.

After I finished my residency in general internal medicine, I opted to stay on at Harborview as an attending—or fully licensed—doctor. I was thirty years old, and at that time, single. I had many reasons for staying on, one of which was that the hospital seemed like a place where people who arrived ill and out of options could genuinely get some help. Equally important was that so many of the physicians were the sort of people I hoped to become. Among these were Michael Copass—a jack of many trades who preached equality but in his heart seemed to most enjoy helping the working poor and the vulnerable—and colorful doctors like nephrologist Pat Fleet, who was known for taking on challenging cases, such as drug addicts who had threatened to kill their previous doctors.

My expectation was that I would work there for a year or two, burn out, and move on with my life. I stayed six years because I fell in love with a story. It is the story of a tough and unique group of human beings who are committed to a vision of equality for the most vulnerable people in our society, a group who believes that everyone should be treated equally and well, regardless of who they are. And it is the story of a unique place that has somehow operated in the black, all the while caring for a charity caseload that has exploded from $43 million in 2002, my first year of attending, to $112 million in 2006.

Harborview's story is in many ways a troubling tale. It is about patients who struggle with chronic illness under conditions that can be downright horrific, patients who cannot always access medical care as quickly or easily as a prudent layperson might deem reasonable. It is a story about gentrification in health services, about the coming appeal to the health care consumer, and the dawn of rationing, especially for new drugs and costly screening tests.

The fact of the matter is that nobody really knows how to best care for the working poor and the indigent; the strategy in recent times has been to minimize one's exposure, since taking care of this population has become so financially damaging. But the people of Harborview are still trying, and in these efforts, I believe, is the story of a place that has the power to transform how we think about commerce and charity, a story that has the potential to heal our outdated ideas about health and poverty.

This is that story.

Life Support

What people always remembered about a man named Dave French was that he lived in a car with four flat tires. Dave was forty-nine years old and had collapsed without warning after withdrawing cash from an automated teller machine. His companion caught him as he fell and tried to rouse him, but Dave was unresponsive when the paramedics arrived a few minutes later, his hands turned a dusky blue color. The medics knelt swiftly, slid a breathing tube in his windpipe, and lifted him onto the ambulance, which whisked him away with moaning sirens.

By the time Dave's gurney rolled through the swinging doors of Harborview's Intensive Care Unit (ICU), the bag ventilator honking and sighing, Dave was in the throes of severe septic shock. He suffered from lung failure, heart failure, liver failure, kidney failure, and he was comatose. He had intestinal bleeding and a systemic infection. His heart ticked along at 150 beats per minute, and his blood pressure plunged repeatedly.

I was the senior medicine resident in the ICU the night that Dave was admitted to the hospital. To treat the low blood pressure, we gave a multiple-liter push of intravenous fluid, and this soon flooded his lungs, impairing

1

oxygen levels. I donned gown and gloves and threaded a catheter down into his heart, to deliver vasopressor medication, which raises blood pressure. The first drug worked for about thirty minutes. By the time I stepped away from the bedside to check in with the attending physician, Dave was receiving three vasopressors at maximum doses. The situation was dire.

At two o'clock in the morning, I phoned Dave's parents. An emergency social worker had somehow tracked down their number. After several rings, a woman who identified herself as Donna French picked up. She was married to Dave's father, she said. I explained that Dave was unconscious and in intensive care. I described the intravenous medications that were keeping him alive. Had she seen him recently?

"We don't see him much. On Thanksgiving he called to say he didn't feel well and couldn't make it. That was the last we heard. It was four or five days ago. He had the stomach flu." Her voice was thin and fragile.

"Thank you, that's helpful," I said. This suggested that Dave's illness had come on somewhat gradually. "Do you know who he could have been with?"

"We don't know his friends," she said. "Should we come in? Because we're a four-hour drive. We could send his brother now. But we can leave here first thing in the morning." Morning would be fine, I said, apologizing for the middle-of-the-night interruption. I would call back if things worsened. But who was I kidding? Things couldn't get much worse for Dave. He was five organ systems down and showed no sign of consciousness. He had cocaine and heroin in his urine, and there was very little left to do should his blood pressure drop again and his heart give out.

The job of the senior ICU resident was to keep patients alive until more experienced minds arrived in the morning and could help sort things through. I had been in the Harborview ICU for nearly a month, and the learning curve had been steep. On my call nights, I had helped to resuscitate some of the sickest patients in the city, and I felt confident that I could keep Dave going until the sun came up. And so, because there was no indication that he would want otherwise, we did everything humanly possible to keep him going.

By mid-morning, Dave's condition had stabilized somewhat, and for the next forty-eight hours, he neither got worse nor really improved. On the evening of his second hospital day, his liver function began to normalize. His intestinal bleeding stopped, and his arms and legs started to move. None of us understood why he'd collapsed, or what had incited the multiple–organ-system failure. The best guess was that he had used some really bad drugs.

On hospital day three, we collected spinal fluid to check for a protein that could predict whether he would ever wake up again. The results indicated that he very likely would, so we pushed onward with aggressive treatment. Soon Dave came off the vasopressor medication. We began feeding him through a stomach tube. His kidneys showed signs of life. Still, though, he remained comatose. Perhaps his brain had been deprived of oxygen after he collapsed, we opined, but brain scans showed no apparent damage.

Dave's father, Sam French, visited every day around lunchtime. Sam was a self-made man who had developed a wildly successful business selling second-pick fruit to companies like Sara Lee, and he and his wife had retired to a ranch on the Olympic Peninsula. Sam was thick-boned and always came dressed in a sport coat and khaki slacks. He would pull a chair to the bed and talk to Dave whenever he thought of something to say, because the nurses said a familiar voice could hasten Dave's recovery.

Sam did not actually believe that Dave could hear him talking. He was impressed by his son's deep coma, and by the number of systems that had malfunctioned. After a few days without much improvement, he began to talk with his wife, Donna, about turning off the machines. His resolve grew, and he told his son and daughter, "I take all responsibility for these decisions." He didn't want Dave's siblings to shoulder any of the terrible burden of ending their brother's life.

The hitch was that Sam was not legally Dave's next of kin. Adult children were considered next of kin in Washington State, which meant that Dave's twenty-one-year-old son, Tyler, was actually his legal decision-maker. Dave and Tyler had met just three times. Sam told us that Tyler could not handle a profound decision like withdrawing his father's life support, since he hardly knew him, and anyway, he was a Marine and off fighting in Afghanistan. On the fifth hospital day, Sam pulled me aside after rounds and said, "What you've done for Dave is truly incredible."

He began shaking his head. He told me that he'd sent Dave to drug rehab dozens of times over the years, and Dave's most recent stay was nearly nine months. Sam frowned and said, "Four days and he was back on the cocaine." I frowned, thinking that Sam knew about the cocaine only because I had disclosed it. Sam said that drug and alcohol addiction was in Dave's genes.

"He was born that way. You get him out of the hospital and I promise this will all happen again. It won't take him long. Dave is only alive today because of good intentions.

I've talked with my kids, Dave's brother and sister, and they think the right thing to do is to keep him comfortable but stop life support."

After a pause I said, "Let me talk with the team." Withdrawing life support because a person used drugs and lived on the street seemed questionable to me; I didn't think that doctors or family members should decide who was worthy of living. The decision of living or dying belonged to the patient, I believed. But this particular patient wasn't in any state to make a decision.

The following morning, Dave's son, Tyler, stepped off a military airplane at Fort Lewis, south of Seattle, and came straight to the hospital. He was a pale, lanky young man with light brown hair, and he wore a camouflage uniform with his last name, SMITH, embroidered over the left breast pocket. He looked young and very frightened, and when I came in the room, he seemed relieved to have a distraction from his father, whose face and hands were so bloated that the skin felt hard to the touch.

"I got on the first plane," Tyler said. His trip had taken fourteen hours. He felt lucky that his unit hadn't shipped yet; they were scheduled to deploy that month. He told me that he hoped to see his father through the illness, and that his commanding officer had given him permission to be away for as long as necessary.

Tyler looked up hopefully and said, "I'd like to get to know my dad."

We convened in the afternoon. Sam and Donna arrived early and made small talk with the social worker. Tyler huddled at the far end of the table. When the attending physician and I entered, Sam jumped to his feet and shook our hands vigorously; his wife smiled warmly and nodded. She wore a silk blouse and low-hanging pearls.

Sam began the meeting by saying, "Tyler cannot make this decision. He does not know his father in any meaningful way."

Tyler was looking at the table. I turned to him. "Can you tell me how you understand your dad's situation?"

"My father is very sick and could die," Tyler said. "But he has a chance of making it."

"Did he tell you what he would want if he was on life support?"

Sam said, "You didn't know your father."

"I was getting to know him," Tyler said.

Sam looked at me and said, "We've talked about this. Dave's care is costing Seattle thousands of dollars. Why should we allow this? He hasn't given a thing to the community in his forty-nine years. He's never held a regular job. If he survives, he'll go right back to drinking and taking drugs. He's a drain on society." Donna smiled blandly and nodded again.

"Please, stop the madness," Sam said.

The attending and I looked at each other. I'd never had a conversation like this before, but I'd also never been in a place where poverty and wealth existed so intensely together, in such close quarters. In my steadiest voice I said, "Some of our patients are addicted to drugs and alcohol. We provide medical care because we believe they deserve a chance."

Sam shook his head.

I continued, "We would recommend withdrawing care if Dave had told someone specifically that he never wanted life support, or if there was objective evidence that he wasn't going to wake up. But his situation doesn't really meet either of those conditions. We think he could come through."

I turned to Tyler again and asked, "Did your father ever tell you he didn't want life support?"

Tyler turned even more pale and said, "No."

"Do you think he'd want the treatment he's getting?"

"I guess I'd want to give him a chance."

Sam threw up his hands in exasperation. "You've heard my opinion. The care is incredible, but misguided."

On the eighth day of hospitalization, the attending and I revisited Dave's situation. It was a day before I would "rotate" off service and begin a new assignment at a hospital across town. Parts of Dave seemed to be on the mend. His kidney function was back to normal. His lungs required modest oxygen support, and he was moving around quite a bit, which meant that his brain was working. But he remained unresponsive, and I mentioned my doubts about the spinal fluid results. Would Dave really wake up? Was he entering a permanent vegetative state? The attending didn't believe so. The spinal fluid test was a very good one, he reminded me. Sometimes it just took a while for patients to come to.

For many months I heard nothing about what happened to Dave, preoccupied as I had become with a new service at a different hospital. I thought once or twice about calling the resident who'd taken over his care but never connected with her. Still, I thought about Dave from time to time, and one afternoon while I was working at the university hospital, I flagged down Denise Dudzinski, a clinical ethicist and associate professor of medical ethics at the University of Washington, to tell her about the case.

She said, "Dave's family seemed to base their decision on what they saw as Dave's social worth, and not on what would benefit him the most. That's why your response was to draw back and try to protect him. You were trying to do what seemed most compassionate for the patient."

She studied my reaction and added, "You don't always have all the information you need. You just try to make the best, most genuine decision you can."

A Case of the Jaws

The following commandments were to be observed at all times in the Harborview Emergency Department (ED):

1. Work hard.

2. Be polite.

3. Treat the patient graciously, even if he is not the president of the United States.

The commandments originated from a long-time Harborview physician named Michael Copass, a neurologist by training and someone who did not appear to have much bite to him. Copass stood somewhat shy of five feet nine and was averse to eye contact. He wore wire-rimmed glasses. He styled his sparse hair in a silvery comb-over, and every day he dressed in the same grandfathery sweater-vest, white shirt, and khaki pants.

In fact Copass had been the mostly benign dictator of emergency operations since the early 1970s, about a decade before emergency medicine was recognized as its own specialty. To work with Copass, as thousands of paramedic and physician trainees had done over the years, was to understand that Copass took the commandments seriously; any breach of protocol might be interpreted as a slight against him. Most recently, Copass had relaxed his grip on patient care in the ED to a crop of younger attending physicians, but nevertheless maintained a ubiquitous presence, perhaps because he continued to orchestrate the monthly trainee orientations, and to run the department's daily morning rounds.

I was scheduled to return to Harborview during my last month of residency, for a rotation in Copass's ED. The ED orientation for me and three other residents began precisely at the scheduled time, when Copass locked the classroom door and illustrated the second commandment by saying, "Thank you in advance for the service you will perform for the county." He was in an expansive mood and began by talking about Seattle's first paramedics and a massive motor home named Moby Pig, the primitive ambulance. The moral of his story? "We try new things because we want to make ourselves better."

A knock interrupted his banter, and his cheerful expression melted away. He set his jaw, marched to the door, and released the bolt, unleashing an icy glare upon the latecomer. The four of us residents made eye contact warily.

Soon we were pressing up against a table of naked mannequins. Copass stood at the head of the table and coached us through the mechanics of CPR, encouraging me to climb up to achieve better leverage for chest compressions. He turned toward the portable defibrillator, reviewed its operation, and we each practiced calling for medications between the simulated shocks and compressions. We needed to get aggressive with our maneuvers, he said.

The real business of the day was a crash course in emergency communications. The center of ED communications was the radio room—a bright, hushed space off the main hallway between the front of the department, where trauma and sick medical patients were treated, and the back of the department, where the less acutely ill patients were triaged. Copass told us we would be summoned to the radio room from time to time by a pager that one of us would carry at all times. Part of the skill was in knowing what to do with the thirteen telephones and numerous radio handsets around the room.

One of the phones would ring about thirty seconds after the page came through, Copass said. The caller was usually an airlift nurse or paramedic, or an operator from the trans-fer center, which was the hospital triage office that screened potential patients from outside hospitals. At the far end of the bank of telephones was a black phone that carried only calls to or from Copass. He clamped his jaw again and said, "Please answer the black phone when it rings," and noth-ing about the ED seemed scarier than the prospect of the Copass phone ringing while you were fumbling around the radio room, getting your bearings.

The pager would ring with an encoded message like "10-T," Copass explained, and you would head in, stetho-scope swinging from your neck, and answer the handset with a greeting such as "This is the Medic One Doctor for Medic Ten."

"Medic Ten for Medic One Doc," the paramedic would say.

"Go ahead please."

"How do you read?"

"Loud and clear."

"We have a sixty-two-year-old male patient of Dr. Fleet's, with shortness of breath. Blood pressure is 215 over 140. Request permission to give intravenous Lasix."

"Copy, you're with a very hypertensive sixty-two-year-old male, agree with the IV Lasix."

"We'll be there in ten minutes."

"Copy, see you when you get here."

"Medic Ten out."

"Medic One Doc out."

Copass smiled thinly and said, "Keep it basic." We were still standing, and I flexed my toes isometrically, to keep blood moving in my feet. When the call was over, we were to activate the walkie-talkie and say, "Medic One Doc to Charge and Triage—sixty-two-year-old male Fleet patient with shortness of breath and BP of 215 over 140 ten minutes out," which would communicate to the charge and triage nurses that the patient was at risk for cardiac arrhythmia, and as a Fleet patient, might need emergency dialysis. By the time you'd finished scribbling out the particulars of the call and were back on the ED floor, the charge nurse had designated a front-of-the-house bed for the incoming patient and was moving its current occupant to a back bay.

Copass told us the paramedics would transport significant trauma, burns, ongoing CPR, drug overdoses, and brain bleeds; these cases came to us no matter what.

"In fact," he said, "if there's any doubt, the answer is 'yes.' As in, 'Yes. Thank you. We'd be delighted to take care of the patient.'"

In case the third commandment was still not clear, Copass began to describe a drinker named Douglas Lightfoot who was routinely delivered to the county ED by the Seattle Police Department. "What's important about Mr. Lightfoot is that he pickled his hypothalamus," Copass said. "Which makes him an amphibian. Put him on a warm rock, he gets warm. Put him on a cold rock, he gets cold. When Mr. Lightfoot comes in, you should say, 'How may I help you, sir? Can I get you a warm blanket? Can I get you some hot soup?' Because that's usually what Mr. Lightfoot needs."

On the occasion that Mr. Lightfoot went to the "wrong" hospital, Copass said, we might find ourselves receiving a cranky call from someone wanting to know why we couldn't take care of our own patients. Copass's crooked grin suggested that this was just the sort of confrontation he favored. "It is a privilege to take care of our patients," he would say. He warned us to not keep Mr. Lightfoot waiting while we got coffee or composed a Pulitzer-worthy chart note. If something needed doing, we were to handle it politely and efficiently and, when we were done, move on to the next patient.

"The essence of the emergency room can be summed up like this: How quickly can we work, how well can we do?"

To understand Copass, you had to know that he was the son of a homemaker and a judge who grew up in the Great Depression. You had to know he was raised in a modest household, that he considered law but opted for medicine, and that he worked five different jobs as a medical student. You had to know that he fought in Vietnam and was honorably discharged with the rank of army major, and above all that when he returned to Chicago, where he'd begun a medicine internship before the draft swept him off, he discovered that the elite hospitals were closed to him and to his coarse brand of wartime medicine.

Embattled and discouraged, the young Copass moved back to Seattle. At that late date, the only thing available was a neurology residency at Harborview. But Copass was so eager to practice medicine again that he agreed to the residency immediately, and while awaiting his start date, he took calls every third night at the busy Firlands Sanatorium, caring for institutionalized tuberculosis patients. He was grateful for every opportunity to gain clinical experience.

He was grateful for the inspired young neurologists he would meet, and then for the year he spent dissecting cadavers' brains with the neuropathologists—a profound process, he said, that crystallized his understanding of human neurologic function.

Copass was so grateful that he decided to stay on at Harborview, giving five years of service to discharge his debts. But the hospital could not afford another neurologist. What the hospital needed was an entrepreneurial person to tackle the problematic emergency room, which was, like every other emergency room in the city then, a busy urgent care center.

Copass took on the ED in 1970, as a golden era in emergency medicine was beginning. The new paramedic operation, Medic One, had gained widespread notoriety after television's *60 Minutes* called Seattle the "best place to have a heart attack." Patients were resuscitated in the field by paramedics, transported rapidly to the hospital, stabilized in the emergency room, and then sent upstairs to a brand-new cardiac ICU. It was a busy time, a heady time, and the amazing result was that one-third of the people who collapsed at home and would previously have been declared dead on-site were now being whisked to Harborview and walking out of the hospital.

Over the years Copass's reach continued to expand. He concocted trauma protocols for the surgery side of the ED and pushed the boundaries of cardiac resuscitation forward on the medicine side. When he saw that young people were dying of traumatic injury and acute medical illness in the outer reaches of the Pacific Northwest, he formed an airlift company to transport patients from remote places to Seattle for definitive care.

But his biggest influence came with his teaching. He instructed medical students, residents, and young faculty on emergency medicine and neurology. He taught pre-hospital care to paramedics and EMTs, and to 20 percent of Seattle's citizens, so that someone who collapsed at work or on the street could be revived, moments later, by a civilian bystander.

At all times, he insisted on strict adherence to his three commandments. The result was that the paramedics were the most polite and effective public servants a person could want, and that Harborview had become a dignified place to receive medical care, no matter who you were.

Under his direction, the Harborview ED grew to be among the busiest in the Pacific Northwest, with 90,000 visits in 2005. Patients suffered from gunshot and stabbing wounds, motor vehicle collisions, burns, attempted suicides, drug overdoses, and every manner of shock and organ failure, and Copass was at the center of the action.

On his belt he wore a small arsenal of pagers plus a walkie-talkie and cell phone to keep in close contact with his clinic patients; the county's paramedic network; the inpatient neurology service; the ED attendings, residents, and medical students; and the emergency aircraft service. He had been known to materialize at ongoing resuscitations on the city fringes, fire out orders, and hop back into his speedy little car. He could sometimes be found in the ED late at night, helping surgery residents to examine a car crash victim for spinal injury.

Copass described himself as merely the retriever for the hospital, fetching and stabilizing complex patients for the stars such as Sig Hansen, a world-renowned foot and ankle surgeon. The assessment was only partially accurate. Under Copass's direction, the ED had become the command center and soul of the hospital, receiving patients from his paramedics and delivering them to the operating rooms, hospital floors, ICUs, psychiatry wards, radiology suites, and echocardiology labs. Functioning under his oft-repeated mantra—How quickly can we work, how well can we do?—the ED steadily filled the hospital with complicated cases: sometimes more cases, in fact, than there were beds.

Even when every bed in the hospital was filled and patients could be found boarding in hallways, in storage areas, and in the holding tank behind the radiology suite, Copass believed that the hospital doors should remain open, particularly for the poor and uninsured—the refugees, prisoners, and injection drug users who had difficulty obtaining care elsewhere. This meant that he routinely clamped his jaw and called up the chiefs of the medical and surgical services, asking if they could please get off their asses and get patients taken care of so that the newest and sickest could have somewhere to lie down.

When the telephone missives failed, he sent junior ED attendings sprinting upstairs to urge discharge of the healthiest patients. Whether this created anything more than friction was hard to say, but the fact was the hospital doors had remained open for many years, through the crush of summer trauma cases that arrived when the weather warmed up, and despite the steadily increasing number of uninsured patients who were flowing through the hospital doors.

Some believed that the system worked because Copass's temper greased the wheels. When he felt a patient had waited too long or received suboptimal care, he sometimes asked, "Do I need to have a fit?" I had once seen him hopping up and down, slamming the soles of his shoes on the radio room floor. More often, though, he lapsed into what he called "a case of the jaws," when he grew grave and silent.

Some people claimed that when he got the jaws, they had seen steam coming out of his ears.

ED rounds took place during the calmest hour in the department, which was usually between six and seven o'clock in the morning. Most of the patients who had received medical care during the previous twenty-four hours had been discharged by then, so the review of the previous day's cases was focused on a stack of charts on the radio room counter. The charts were really two pieces of paper stapled together: a face sheet listed the patient's contact information, mode of travel to the ED, insurance status, and primary physician. The second page abstracted the medical concern and plan. Rounds got under way as soon as Copass gathered up his red grease pencils, pulled off a few shavings, sharpened the pencil points, and then positioned himself alongside the chart pile. We clustered around and behind him, and he began to narrate the previous day's patients.

"Jessie Bouvier. Comes to us with a bit of the gonorrhea. How many people is she sleeping with every day?" He looked to one of the medical students, who turned up her palms.

He continued, "Maybe a dozen. Probably a half-dozen." He flipped the page, aimed his red grease pencil, and underlined the urine toxicology result, which was positive for opiates, heroin, cocaine, methamphetamines, and PCP. He said, "What's happening here is a little trade. She wants the cocaine, she makes a deal with men who can help her. She sleeps with a half-dozen, and how many do you think the half-dozen are sleeping with?" The student shook her head. "How about three or four apiece. So how many people get exposed to the gonorrhea?"

He lowered his voice a few notes and said, "You ever heard of Anna, Illinois? Only reason I know about Anna, Illinois, is because my college roommate is from Anna, Illinois, and I went there to see him get married. A lot of truckers come through Anna, Illinois. And they had their eye on one lady who slept with a trucker coming through Anna, Illinois, who happened to have gonorrhea. How many people do you think were infected along the way from Anna, Illinois, to Los Angeles, where the trucker ended his job? Six hundred thirty-four. All from one woman in Anna, Illinois, and a trucker. So what are we going to do for this nice young lady who comes here for care?"

He paused a couple beats, made a few marks on the patient's chart, and underlined the doxycycline that the resident had prescribed.

"Message left for health department," he read.

He flipped to the next chart and said, "A sixty-year-old Filipino lady with schizophrenia." He turned to me. "Did you ever hear of a Filipino with schizophrenia? I never did. It doesn't exist. They hear things, they see things, but they don't get schizophrenia." He marked the chart note randomly with his red grease pencil as he scanned what was written. He continued, "All Filipinos are healthy until the age of eighty-five. Which is remarkable, because the primary calorie in their diet is salt." I barely suppressed a laugh.

"Next is our old friend Walter Eddy, at 1824 Second Avenue South. Now that's an interesting address. Last time I was driving up Second Avenue South, number 1824 was a vacant lot with overgrown ragweed and a mailbox. So why use a vacant lot for your address? Does that sound like a good idea?"

He paused. "Maybe Walter needs somewhere he can receive his monthly check. So why not the mailbox at 1824?"

Copass turned to the second page. "A heart rate of 110, a temperature of 102. That's probably real. Does he have a cough? Does he have a white count? Ah, an opacity in the LLL. Ceftriaxone and azithromycin. Admit to medicine."

He circled the X-ray result, underlined "pneumonia," and wrote "AMC" in thick red letters across the patient's face sheet, for the Adult Medicine clinic, so that the chart would be routed to Walter's doctor. Copass flipped to the next chart, which was a patient I had taken care of sometime after midnight: "Peter Ogrinc. Lives at 513 Third Avenue. Do you know where that is, 513 Third Avenue?"

I said, "I'm sorry, I thought he was homeless."

"Yes, but Mr. Ogrinc lists his address as 513 Third, which is the Downtown Emergency Services Center. The DESC." I folded my hands together. Copass flipped the page and said, "Brought in courteously by the Seattle P.D. for acting oddly. Diabetes out of control. Not unusual for Mr. Ogrinc. Not unusual at all. Was his insulin stolen? Did he lose his psychotropics? Did he forget to eat? Was he flat-out drunk? Mr. Ogrinc has a lot going on sometimes. Is he banned from the DESC?"

Copass underlined the patient's alcohol level. I told him I didn't know the specifics of his mental illness treatment or where he was sleeping.

"So what are we going to do for this gentleman today? We'll refill his insulin and send him to the good Dr. Sugg at Pioneer Square." Copass placed a checkmark next to the insulin prescription and the follow-up appointment I'd requested, then moved to the next chart. I was disappointed Copass hadn't asked any more questions, and only later did I realize he knew I could treat diabetes. What he was trying to teach had to do with the person.

Late in my month, a tall, thin Ethiopian named Chep entered the hospital at Ninth and Jefferson, passed through the metal detector, and approached the ED desk. Chep was having pain over his shoulder blade. The triage nurse took his vitals—the pulse was slightly fast—and sent him to a gurney in the back hallway, then wrote "low back pain" on the board.

I put Chep on my mental back burner, since ED patients with nocturnal back pain typically just wanted narcotics. But it eventually became clear that everyone else was putting him off too, including the medical students, who were generally eager to take on whoever walked in the door. Finally I picked up Chep's blank chart. Copass would have a fit, I knew, when he saw the three-hour waiting time. It wouldn't matter that the diagnosis was back pain, that the patient just wanted drugs, that I hadn't had a sip of water in seven hours.

Chep was sitting at the edge of the gurney, and it seemed that his legs stretched halfway across the hall. I'd passed him several times already, on my way to care for other patients, and now I felt bad for putting him off.

"I'm sorry for the delay," I said. "You have back pain?" It wasn't the best way to start a conversation, but it was almost four o'clock in the morning.

"Not really," he said. He had been walking in a park three days before, he said, when something tore in his chest and he became breathless. He touched under his collarbone where the pain had come on. The breathing problem had gotten worse, and now he could walk only a few steps. I asked if it was painful to take a deep breath, and he said, "I can't take a deep breath." I began to hurry through the story. Any other medical problems? No. Medications? None. Do you smoke? Yes, he said sheepishly.

I reached for my stethoscope in the pocket of my white coat, and he twisted around. His lung sounds were muffled under the right shoulder blade, and his heart sounded faint and far away.

"We'll get an X-ray," I said. I would finish examining him after the X-ray was done. "It's possible that your lung has collapsed."

"I think so," he said.

I found the attending physician and related the story. She glanced at the whiteboard, where "low back pain" was written beside the patient's name, and said, "Really?" She studied the patient from a distance. "He looks well."

We watched Chep walk into the radiology suite, a dimly lit cavern between the bright front and back hallways.

"I know he looks comfortable, but he's got a really good story," I said. *And maybe he did have a minor back strain*, I thought, and sat down to write the note in the charting area, called the Fishbowl. I realized I had no idea what he did for work or whether he had insurance. If a chest tube was required, he would have to be hospitalized, and could be paying off medical bills for years to come. A few minutes later the night resident came running out of the radiology cavern.

"Is this your patient?" he said, holding the black-and-white image up to the light. The left half of Chep's chest was empty. "It's a large pneumo—compressing the heart."

"Nice call," someone said. I looked around the Fishbowl and saw Copass standing at one of the desks behind me. Where had he come from? A nurse folded Chep into a wheelchair and rushed him to an open bed in the front resuscitation suite. I turned away, hoping Copass wouldn't notice Chep's intake time, posted on the whiteboard, which showed how long we had ignored the potentially life-threatening illness.

The lead trauma doctor had already heard about the collapsed lung from the radiologists, and I talked with him about placing a chest tube to reinflate the lung. When I popped back into the Fishbowl a few minutes later, Copass still hadn't budged from his spot. He was preoccupied with a tall stack of paper, and I realized that he was just about to start reviewing the previous day's charts. He quietly asked me, "Why aren't you putting the chest tube in? You should put it in if you want to. He's your patient."

"I would like to."

Copass motioned to the surgery resident and told him the intern would have to wait for the next try. In a moment I was pulling on sterile gloves. The X-ray hung from the light board next to Chep's bed. I explained to him that I was going to numb up his skin and place a tube to drain the air in his chest, which would require making an incision near the base of his rib cage. He would be awake while we did the procedure.

"Thank you," he said. "How did this happen?"

I drew lidocaine into a syringe, tapped it to dislodge air bubbles, and injected the medication under his skin. "Tall, thin young men will sometimes get a collapsed lung for no good reason," I said. Apparently this made sense to him because he nodded and then said, "I am going to quit smoking."

"Good idea."

"Will it happen again?"

"It doesn't to most people." We rolled him into position, I drew a small incision with the scalpel, and the surgery resident instructed me to push deeply with my fingers. I felt the firm chest muscles and hard curve of the rib, then began to open the fascia and muscle with forceps. The surgery resident looked as though he wanted to take the tools himself, so I pushed harder until I was leaning my whole body weight into the forceps. Finally the metal popped through the moist silvery tissue with a rip, and warm air hissed out.

"Ohhh," Chep said, exhaling. He hadn't flinched once during the uncomfortable procedure. The resident helped me feed thick tubing, about the caliber of a garden hose, into Chep's chest.

"That feels better," Chep said. I stitched the tube in, washed up, and headed for the radio room, where Copass was halfway through the medicine charts. Almost eagerly he said, "You put it in?" I smiled automatically, and he said, "Good work." He resumed his rhythmic chatter about the patients, about the places they roamed and where the medics picked them up, as though they were a wild species he was tracking by radio collar.

With the pile depleted, the crowd began to scatter. Copass indicated that I should stay put, and when the radio room was otherwise empty, he turned to face me, a pale, embattled warrior with his belt of pagers and cell phones, arbiter of etiquette and champion of the vulnerable.

"What's your start date?" He had heard, then, that I was coming to Harborview to practice medicine after I finished residency training the following week. I would be based on the wards upstairs, taking care of sick patients admitted to the medicine service after the residents had reached their daily limit.

I told him I would start the day after residency ended, which gave me about a twenty-four-hour window away from the hospital, but I didn't complain to him about this.

He said, "Young doctors in this hospital once knew how to take care of whoever came through the door. Young doctors in this hospital never used to say no." I couldn't see whether his cheek was twitching or not.

I nodded.

"This can be a difficult place. It can be frustrating. If there is ever something I can help you with, please let me know." He reached out to shake my hand.

"Thank you," I said, and practically floated out of the radio room.

On the Wards

Home base for my new job was the medicine ward, which was the third and fourth floors of the old hospital building. Three and Four were vintage wards with wide, breezy hallways and twelve-foot ceilings. Most of the patient rooms were semi-private, with two hospital beds, a spartan metal sink and shared bathroom, and enormous windows, some of which provided territorial views of the Puget Sound and the downtown skyscrapers. On the medicine wards, only those who were highly infectious or about to pass away got a private room.

In the core of the ward was the nursing station, a social work office, a satellite pharmacy, and two doctor work areas, as well as laundry and supply rooms and a pantry. At the center of the action was the floor ward clerk, who often knew what was happening before anybody else did, owing to her multiplicity of tasks: answering the ever-ringing phones, entering physicians' orders into the computer, announcing codes on the intercom, and directing traffic for patients and their families, who were eternally coming and going.

My new office was thirty paces off of Four, in a quiet spot just beyond the flow of foot traffic. Historically the room had been used for patient care, but in the 1960s it had been declared unfit to withstand a serious earthquake. More recently it had been a work area for medicine residents on assignment at the hospital, and on my first day the long desk was piled high with journal articles, discarded physician order sheets, tuberculosis hoods, and half-used boxes of bright blue nitrile gloves. There were two outdated desktop computers, a pair of large running shoes on one of the desk chairs, and a green vinyl couch on the far side of the room. There was also a small bathroom lined with beige tile and a cord, hanging from the wall, that could be pulled in emergencies. I folded my arms. With a big cleanup job, plus a throw and pillows for the couch, the place might actually be kind of cozy.

After surveying the space, I headed upstairs to buff and polish my employment paperwork, which would establish my various hospital privileges and billing identification numbers. The administrator told me that the division still required signatures of approval from the department of medicine chair, the medical school dean, and the university president before I could see patients again, and certainly before I could get paid. She brandished a silver notary stamp, which did the job with a ruthless little crunch. "Getting this done is usually a three-month process," she said, smiling with all of her teeth.

In the middle of the morning, I attended a meeting with the professional fee coders, who generated bills from doctors' chart notes; this was the first instruction I'd ever gotten in the business of medicine. The coders wore skirt suits and eye shadow and were as unflappable as dog trainers. They offered cheerful homilies like, "Remember, billing isn't about what you did for the patient! Billing is about what you write down." The government health insurance plan, Medicare, had again changed its documentation rules, and the veteran doctors in attendance were grumpy with questions, which the coders dispatched with polite but firm voices.

Afterward I headed back to Four, swept the clutter of my new office into thick garbage bags, and phoned housekeeping for a pickup. I left the running shoes in the ED, where a homeless patient might pick them up, and took off for lunch. In the afternoon, the administrator paged with the news that the signatures were all in. I would start in the morning.

My new job title was attending physician in general internal medicine. I would be working on the medicine side of the hospital, where the stories were about the gradual erosion of living. I would interact very little, at least in the beginning, with Harborview's camera-ready surgery side, where stories often began with a gunfight, a house fire, or a bucking horse. On a typical morning not long after I'd begun my new job, another brand-new attending named Alice Brownstein was working in the ED, and she was anxious for me to admit three patients to the hospital for further care. I walked downstairs. Alice was in the Fishbowl, scribbling a note. She was thirty-something and had flaxen hair, blue eyes, and a healthy tan, having just returned from riding her bicycle 3,157 miles from Seattle to her mother's home in Washington, D.C., to celebrate the completion of medical training. Her trip stats included thirteen states, six flat tires, one broken spoke fixed with duct tape, twenty-seven orders of bacon, and eight tubes of sunscreen.

Alice shuffled the notes in front of her and began to tell me the "bullet" on each of the three new patients. First was Mirabelle Fleming, a thirty-year-old woman with bad lung disease, who was swollen all over and couldn't breathe. Second was Marvin Hooley, a homeless drinker with sweats and fevers, who hadn't kept anything down in a couple of days. "Nice guy," Alice said. And third was Kermit Jackson, a forty-two-year-old "friend of Fleet" who went by the nickname Agent K.

"The nursing home says he missed his last two runs. Told them he was too sick to go. So Potassium is 6.9 and Renal is in there with him now." This was shorthand to indicate that the kidney doctors were preparing for urgent dialysis.

Alice smiled and added, "Oh, and just an FYI. He threatened to kill both me and the nurses. Good luck with that."

"Excellent," I said. "He's forty-two years old and lives in a nursing home?"

"Right now he does. He bounces around," she said.

I found Kermit first. He was lying in his gurney with the hood of his sweatshirt hanging over his eyes and blankets pulled up to his mouth. Only his nostrils were visible. Under the covers his head nodded rhythmically. The dialysis nurse was checking the long cords that carried blood between a catheter implanted in Kermit's chest and the dialysis machine, a tall box that resembled a robot on wheels.

"Mr. Jackson," I said. Kermit did not seem to hear me. "Mr. Jackson, can you talk to me?" I leaned in and touched his shoulder.

"Hey!" he screamed. "Don't touch me!" The dialysis nurse gave me a knowing look.

I lifted the sweatshirt off Kermit's forehead and his eyes snapped open. He wore an enormous pair of headphones.

"Don't touch me or I will kill you!"

I introduced myself as the hospital doctor, and Kermit stared. "Naw. Fleet is my doctor," he said.

"Of course, I'll be consulting with Dr. Fleet."

"Fleet already came by."

"Listen, Fleet does your kidney stuff, and I do everything else. So I just need some information from you. Can you tell me why you missed dialysis?"

Kermit turned up his music so that I could hear the beat pounding through the headphones.

"All right," I said. "I have to listen to your heart." I unraveled my stethoscope and aimed for his chest, but he batted me away. My hands shaking, I circumnavigated the bed, hoping to get a glimpse of the dialysis catheter. When I reached for the covers, he yanked them up.

I stood for a moment, watching him move defiantly to his music.

"Nice to meet you," I said, doubting he heard me. I wasn't sure how anybody could figure out what was the matter with him, so I turned away, found his chart, and ordered blood and urine cultures, a chest X-ray, and an echocardiogram, hoping that tests might provide some answers.

I headed for Mirabelle Fleming's room, down the hall from Kermit. She wasn't there, so I went searching for Marv Hooley, whose presence hadn't registered with the hospital computers yet. Eventually I found him in the back of the ED, where he was snoring loudly on a gurney. I shook his shoulder to wake him up. He was a sodden lump.

"Sir, you're at the hospital."

"Lord!"

"Can you please wake up?"

"Sorry." His eyes opened.

"How do you feel?"

"Better!" he said eagerly. His gown was damp and the creases of his palms were dark with grime.

"When was your last drink?"

"Yesterday." I noted that his hands were trembling.

"How much do you drink?"

"A fifth a day."

"Did you eat anything today?"

"I been throwing up."

"Look, you have heart failure. We'll put you in the hospital and make sure you didn't have a heart attack."

"You think I had a heart attack?" Marv was awake now and pushing himself up to a sitting position. "I don't think I had a heart attack."

"We'll find out. We'll keep you in the hospital two or three days and try to get you feeling better."

"Thank you, ma'am," he said, and dropped back to sleep immediately. The nursing notes in his folder said he had passed out in a doorway downtown, that he had been picked up during a routine sweep of the streets. The blood test results showed no evidence yet of heart attack; the blood alcohol level was 295 milligrams per deciliter, or .295, almost four times the legal limit for drivers. He was going to withdraw from the high alcohol level, so I wrote orders for intravenous benzodiazepines to prevent seizure, and for vitamins. But what he really needed, I decided, was a high-calorie diet. He was just so skinny.

Mirabelle was still out of her room when I returned to Three, and a nurse passing by told me she was downstairs having a smoke.

"I thought she was having trouble breathing."

The nurse smiled. "I suppose she feels better."

"Right." My pager rang. It was Kermit's nurse calling to tell me that he had refused the X-ray and urinalysis, and she didn't think he'd agree to the echocardiogram. I called her back a moment later when I saw that his blood cultures were growing a gram-positive bug, which suggested an infection of the heart valve.

"So maybe you could talk to him about why that's such an important test," she said.

"Sure," I said, knowing that the conversation was not likely to go well. I would probably just piss him off some more and not actually change his mind.

Then I heard Pat Fleet's gravelly, musical voice coming from a workroom in the ward core and found him holding forth on sodium balance with a cluster of residents and fellows. Fleet had dark, intelligent eyes and a great mop of hair, and he wore a plaid shirt, khaki pants, and leather sandals. As I sat down, Fleet wrapped up his mini-lecture, turned to me, and said hello. I introduced myself as one of the new attendings and said I'd just met Kermit Jackson.

"Welcome to Harborview," Fleet said. "Did Kermit threaten to kill you?"

"He did, in fact."

"Well, that's his M.O. when he's off the meds," Fleet said. He was talking about Kermit's psychiatric medication. "Talented horn player, by the way. You might ask him about that."

I started shaking my head. "He's not interested in talking to me and didn't let me examine him. So that's a challenge. And there are gram-positive cocci in his blood."

Fleet crossed his arms. "The line's going to have to come out." He meant Kermit's dialysis catheter.

"I wasn't able to look at it, unfortunately."

"Pus everywhere. This is his third infection. We should have pulled it last time but he talked me out of it. I want to run him again in the morning, then yank it."

"Sounds good," I said, even though it did not sound good at all. Kermit would have to stay in the hospital until the bloodstream infection cleared and a new sterile catheter was implanted. There wasn't a way for him to receive dialysis otherwise.

Fleet shrugged and said, "You'll see. The guy is all bark and no bite."

I read Mirabelle's medical chart while waiting for her to return. Her seven-year-old daughter lived in foster care, I learned, and she herself stayed at a homeless women's shelter. She had been intubated and on life support in the ICU the previous month, and critical care doctors had opined that her particular affliction, pulmonary hypertension, was caused by her drug habit, specifically from the small blood clots that developed when a person injected street drugs. Continuing to inject would bring on a rapid end, they'd warned her. Heart-and-lung transplantation was sometimes offered as life-sustaining therapy for those with end-stage pulmonary hypertension, but the selection of "appropriate" candidates for a limited number of organs could resemble the application process at elite colleges. Mirabelle, everyone believed, did not make the grade.

The nurse paged me when Mirabelle finally returned. I hustled over to the ward and stopped in the doorway. She was sitting in bed, sipping a drink through a straw, and she was strikingly pretty. Her long, healthy hair and clean skin didn't fit with homelessness and chronic drug use. The only hint that something was amiss was the plastic tubing that curled over her ears and blew oxygen to her nose. The tap had been turned to six liters per minute, more than many patients with end-stage emphysema used. I said that the emergency doctor had told me about her difficulty breathing.

"I'm so puffy everywhere," she said. "I had to take off my rings." She showed me that her fingers were plump as breakfast sausages. "You're not allowed to sleep sitting up at the shelter, and when I lie down I feel like I'm drowning."

"How far can you walk?"

"I used to go as much as I needed, but I get tired now."

"Do you take medication?"

"I ran out last week."

"What have the doctors told you?"

"They said there's a problem with my heart and my lungs."

"Okay, that's right."

"I haven't shot up in, like, four months. I'm trying to get my daughter back."

I nodded approvingly. "We'll use diuretics to take fluid off your lungs. If you've stopped injecting, the pulmonary hypertension can be reversed."

She shook her head and said, "No one believes I quit."

"It takes a long time for blood vessels to heal after you inject drugs. Sometimes it takes years."

"Years? Are you kidding me?" she said. She asked for something for her chest pain and anxiety, and said, "And I'm allergic to Demerol, Toradol, and ibuprofen."

"I'll have the nurse bring some Tylenol."

"I used to shoot three grams of heroin a day," she said gravely, "so I don't even feel that stuff."

"Tylenol works differently than heroin or narcotics."

She raised an eyebrow and said, "I have pain when I get short of breath." She started to describe how painful her pain was.

I sighed. "I'll write for some oxycodone," I said. Oxycodone was the hospital's basic oral narcotic.

"Thank you for understanding, Doctor. I won't need that when I feel better."

In her chart I ordered a urine drug screen, since she'd made such a big deal about it.

In the afternoon I met for rounds with Barbara Parlotz, a veteran social worker who had been at Harborview for twenty years. Barb's career at the hospital had started with neurosurgery; from there she had gone to the ICU, then to clinic, and then into the administrative ranks, where she realized she preferred patient care. In recent years she had worked with medicine patients on Three and Four, who had presented her with just about every story, sequel, and scam imaginable. She wore jewel-tone suits with smart accessories, carried a ubiquitous binder with her patients' vital stats, and she affected a show-me-the-money approach with both the clientele and the doctors.

At the beginning of our rounds, Barb said, "I see that Kermit Jackson is back."

I was sitting on the green vinyl couch in the office, ready with notes about the new patients. Barb told me she had already helped orchestrate two hospital discharges for Kermit in recent months. I told her about the current bloodstream infection, his potential need for several weeks of intravenous antibiotics.

"His nursing home may refuse to take him back. We really had to beg last time," she said.

"He seems paranoid. I consulted Psychiatry about his meds, which he has refused to take for the last couple of weeks. He may require an inpatient stay on Five." The locked psychiatry wards were located on Five.

"I'll keep the nursing home updated."

"Next is Mirabelle Fleming. Young woman with pulmonary hypertension that may improve if she stops using. She stays at the women's shelter."

Barb read from her binder: "Has a kid in foster care. That's a pretty unusual story." She told me there was generally a lot of government support for mothers with children.

"She says she quit shooting. She wants the kid back."

"That poor kid. And I don't mean the patient."

I pulled up a computer screen showing Mirabelle's urine tox screen, which was negative this time, but I noticed that a screen done in the ED two weeks previous had been positive for heroin and cocaine. I pointed Barb to these results.

"So her pulmonary situation may not be so reversible. But there must be some sort of therapy we could offer."

Barb glanced down at her binder and said, "She doesn't have the right kind of funding to go straight into inpatient drug treatment. I can give her a list of drug treatment resources. We'll get her on the waiting list and follow up when a spot opens."

"That's all we can do?"

"That's it," Barb said. "She's got to start making some better choices."

"Okay," I said. "Third is Marv Hooley, homeless, a drinker, lives at the mission. Marv has heart failure, probably from drinking." Barb scribbled down his diagnoses.

"Will he withdraw?"

"Probably."

"Back to the mission in maybe two or three days?"

"Probably."

"Thank you," Barb said, finishing her notes. "I'll get on the horn."

Before I left for the day, I stopped in to see Kermit Jackson again. He was lying on his back and mumbling when I came in. "My lunch was poisoned," he told me angrily. "My nurse is trying to poison me! Can you believe that shit?"

"I don't think the nurse had anything to do with your lunch. The food comes from the cafeteria service."

Kermit muttered, "I don't know what you're so scared of."

"Excuse me?"

Kermit looked at me suspiciously and said, "Who are you?"

"I'm your doctor."

"Fleet is my doctor."

"Yeah. Fleet is your kidney doctor. I'm the hospital doctor. We talked about it this morning."

"I know," he snapped.

"Listen, you've got an infection in your blood."

"That is what I have been trying to tell you people this whole time! My blood is being poisoned."

"Which is why you're getting antibiotics with dialysis," I said. "But we also need to figure out how long to treat the infection, and to do that I'd like to get an ultrasound of your heart."

"Fuck that," he said.

I sighed and said, "Maybe later, then. Is there anything you need right now?"

"Yeah. I need to talk to the president of the hospital about the fact that I am being poisoned."

"Let me see if I can find someone to come talk with you. It might not be the hospital president. You know, do you ever hear voices or see things?"

"No," Kermit said.

"Could you let me know if that does happen to you?"

"Quiet!" Kermit screamed, looking toward the curtain. His roommate's bed was vacant.

"I'll see you in the morning, Mr. Jackson."

"Thank you for coming by," he said.

"You're welcome. See you in the morning."

At morning signout, the overnight resident led with news of Mirabelle's 1 a.m. oxygen desaturation. The resident said she placed a face mask on the patient and blasted 100 percent oxygen, said it felt like it took forever for her oxygen saturation to come up from the 70s, though it was probably just a few minutes.

"I thought she might need to be intubated," the resident said. "So we talked. She wants everything. Breathing machine, lines, pressors, CPR. I guess I would too. Thirty years old. She got better with face mask oxygen and an extra shot of furosemide. She isn't a transplant candidate, is she?"

"She's young and wants to quit using and has a seven-year-old," I said. I didn't know why I was taking Mirabelle's side. "But you're right. The transplant folks won't even talk to her until she's proven to be clean for six months."

The resident reported that Marv's temperature had hit 103 degrees Fahrenheit, that he'd pulled out his IV and stumbled in the bathroom, bruising his hand on the sink. There were no broken bones on the X-rays.

"He's pretty out of it," she said. She had his wrists and waist tied to the bed so he wouldn't get up and hurt himself again. "He's getting four of lorazepam every couple hours. Is there a limit on how much benzos he can get?"

"He's tachycardic and hypertensive, so he needs all the drugs he's getting. You just have to keep giving more until the vital signs normalize."

"I worry that he'll get so much that he stops breathing."

"Sometimes you have to give that much," I said, and the resident looked horrified. "When that happens, you send them to the ICU to get through it. Sometimes they have to be intubated. But you're trying to keep him from seizing, and he could die if he develops delirium tremens. Right?"

"I see," the resident said. She still seemed skeptical.

Nothing newsworthy had happened with Kermit overnight, to my surprise, and there were two new patients for me to admit that morning: an HIV-positive man with purple hair and a cough, and an elderly woman with an asthma exacerbation, which brought my "service" to eight patients. The computer showed that the new ones were both on Four, so I thanked the resident for her good care, pulled on my white coat, and headed for the wards.

My first stop was to see Mirabelle, who was sleeping peacefully, the hospital bed bent so that she was sitting nearly upright. Oxygen misted around her mouth and nose, and she looked comfortable. I murmured hello and placed my stethoscope over her chest, listening to the coarse lung sounds, then whispered that I'd return when she was awake. A steaming breakfast tray waited on her bedside table, untouched.

Next door, Marv smelled worse than the previous day and was talking incoherently. I examined him and decided on the day's plan: more benzos, supplemental electrolytes to replace what he'd lost, and a moderate amount of IV fluid, since he had heart failure. He hadn't touched his pancakes either, I noticed, but then his hands were tied to the bed.

I stopped in to meet the woman with asthma, whose name was Thelma Smith. Thelma's first question was whether or not she could go: "Honey, I feel 100 percent better."

Thelma told me that she took care of her adult son at home, that he had kidney failure, that she worried about him, so she needed to be on her way as soon as she could. "This all happened because I ran out of my medication."

"You take care of him," I said, "but you're not taking care of yourself."

"I know," she sighed. The chart put her age at seventy-two years old.

"Do you need help at home? Do you need someone to bring meals?"

"Honey, I don't think so," she said.

I told her that she could leave if she could walk without running out of breath, if she promised to visit her regular doctor next week.

"Oh, yes!" she said.

Across the ward was the young man with spiky purple hair, a chatty fellow who said that he hadn't visited a doctor in years, that he'd been healthy, and his HIV had never given him any problems. He worked nights in a convenience mart, and because of his erratic schedule he sometimes forgot to take his antiretrovirals, so the infectious disease doctors had told him to stop taking the meds. He hadn't really thought he needed them in the first place, he said. I told him that the doctors may have been concerned about drug resistance, since he was skipping doses every now and then. The infectious disease doctors said it was healthier in the long run not to take the drugs than to take them 85 percent of the time.

But blood work from earlier in the morning suggested that he had only a few white blood cells left, meaning he was susceptible to a number of otherwise harmless bugs that lived in the soil and water, as well as ordinary fungi and molds. His temperature was 101 degrees. I asked him to bring up something from deep in his lungs and noted that in the meantime he would get speculative treatment for pneumocystis, the classic AIDS pneumonia, a little bug that was maybe fungus and maybe protozoa and could provoke massive lung inflammation.

Finally, I couldn't put off Kermit any longer. Before visiting, I read the psychiatrists' note, a five-page epic. The note commented on Kermit's grooming (dirty street clothes), his speech (pressured), his thought pattern (tangential) and content (homicidal). There was a verbatim quote in the chart: "I am being poisoned! If you don't leave I will kill you!"

The psychiatrists recommended that he resume his previous antipsychotic medication, starting at the lowest dose and increasing over a few days, and that we use Valium by intravenous push if he was out of control. In all, it was not very helpful. I couldn't force Kermit to receive treatment, because he was assumed to be a rational adult, and I personally was not going to stand next to him until he swallowed his pills. I snapped the chart closed and headed for Kermit's room. He was livid.

"I ain't crazy!" he screamed.

"Nobody says you're crazy," I said, clasping my hands. It was all I could do to not cross my arms.

"I don't need no fucking shrink!" he screamed, louder. His face was reddening.

"You've been off your meds."

"You ever take that shit yourself? It really fucks you up."

"Kermit."

"It *makes* you crazy." He was still shouting.

"Look, you have a bad infection. You got really sick when you went off your meds."

His eyes widened and he yelled, "I am not crazy!" A nurse walking by asked if I needed help, and I waved her off. "It's not your fault," I said.

"Look, it really sucks that you're sick," I said.

He grumbled and pulled up his covers.

"I know it's not fair."

He didn't respond, and I wondered if he would switch his music on again so he didn't have to talk with me.

"I know you've been in and out of the hospital since you were nineteen."

"Yeah," he mumbled.

"You know, Fleet mentioned that you play the horn." I said.

Kermit squinted at me and suddenly the normal switch went on. "Yeah. Twenty years. I'm good. I play at all the clubs," he said.

"That's what Fleet said. He said you were really good."

"I'm really good," he said. "You want to buy my CD? I can make you a special deal."

I smiled. "I would be interested in hearing your music sometime," I said. I was feeling almost desperate enough to purchase a patient's affection, too. Before the conversation could change again, I asked if he would let me examine him, and this time he agreed. When I reached gently under his shirt, I saw that his dialysis catheter was crusted over with a gray-green substance.

"It's infected," I said.

"Yeah, it needs to come out," he said.

I decided that I had pushed as far I needed to, that it was enough right now for Kermit to be talking to me and letting me touch him. Next time I would talk with him about the echocardiogram, which he'd already refused twice. While I soaped up at the sink, Fleet zoomed in and said, "What's the matter? I hear you don't like your medications."

"Fuck," Kermit said. "They put me to sleep."

Fleet said, "Yeah, your last dose might have been too high. But you need something."

"I don't know," Kermit frowned.

When I swung past to see Mirabelle again, she was finishing her breakfast, and she was quite pleased with the service she was receiving: "The swelling is down. I can actually see my face."

"Rough night?"

"I have a hard time breathing every night."

"How is your pain?"

"It's gone, and I just want to thank you for listening to me. A lot of doctors don't want to deal with pain. They don't really want to help you out."

"We talked about how you quit using."

"That's right."

"So the urine tox was negative yesterday, as you told me it would be, but two weeks ago it was positive for heroin and cocaine. What's the deal?"

She gave a pretty smile. "Look, I know this lung thing won't get better unless I stay clean. That was a slipup, and I really regret it."

I sighed and told her that I was going to call Pulmonary today, to see what else might be offered for her disease, and then my pager rang. I headed out to the workrooms to answer the call, which was about Thelma, whose oxygen level dropped to 89 percent when she went to the bathroom.

"She can't go home," I said. I hung up and paged Pulmonary. While I was waiting, I began writing the day's chart notes, starting with Marv, who had the easiest plan of all of the patients. Pulmonary called back, and I could hear the doctor tapping at a computer on the other end as I described Mirabelle's story.

"This will kill her," he said. *Click, click.*

"I thought you might have something to recommend in the interim."

"You've got her on the right meds," he said. "Diuretic during the hospitalization, calcium channel blocker chronically. We probably won't have much else to add. She's a shooter, which means she's not a candidate for bosentan." Bosentan was an intravenous drug that cost approximately $10,000 a year and extended life by about six months. The problem wasn't the cost of the drug, as it happened, because the manufacturer would provide it on a charity basis. The

problem was that the drug required a permanent intravenous line so the medication could be infused straight to her
heart. *Primum non nocere*, first do no harm. A permanent
line was just too much temptation for a shooter.

Pulmonary said, "Can you convince her to use oxygen at
home? That may slow down the disease."

I reminded Pulmonary that she was homeless, that the
medical supply company wouldn't lend out a tank unless
the patient had an address. I had learned from Barb, the
social worker, that oxygen tanks usually got damaged or
lost on the streets.

"The patient says she's quit injecting."

"That would certainly be better for her than anything we
can offer."

"Maybe your team can comment on what she would need
to do to get transplanted."

Pulmonary laughed a cruel, patronizing laugh and said,
"Sure. We'll comment on that, too."

I hung up the phone thinking about how arrogantly the
word "certainly" could come off, as in "we are certainly not
going to fix this." Barb was right about Mirabelle: unless
she made up her mind and quit drugs for good, unless
she decided that she wanted to live, she would die within
months. There wasn't much else I could do to help her.

By the end of the week, Marv Hooley started to wake
from his alcohol withdrawal stupor. Mirabelle was feeling a little bit more like her old self, and took leave of the
ward for hours at a time, returning, it seemed, only when
her lips were blue. Pulmonary opined that there was nothing else to be done for her beyond the medications she was
getting already, and then assured me she was not a transplant
candidate and for all intents and purposes never would be.

I discharged Thelma home to tend to her son, but remained perplexed by the HIV patient with purple hair. There was no infection to be found, and yet he continued to grow increasingly breathless. Psychiatry agreed with me that Kermit Jackson appeared incapable of making decisions for himself, that he didn't understand the consequences of not taking antipsychotic medication. Kermit demonstrated that he was resourceful enough, however, to have a medium-size sausage and hot pepper pizza delivered to his room on Three, which he downed in one satisfied sitting. Afterward, when Fleet and I came in to talk with him, he sat in bed smiling like the Cheshire cat.

"When I said you could eat a little bit more, I'm not sure I meant an entire sausage pizza," Fleet said. He studied the box lid and said, "How was it?"

"It was delicious," Kermit said, and smacked his lips.

Fleet shook his head. "Well, we'll see if we can undo the damage a bit when we dialyze you."

On Friday morning, security escorted Kermit to the county's involuntary treatment court across the street from the hospital, where he refused to acknowledge the attorney appointed to argue his case. My affidavit in regard to Kermit Jackson ran to five hundred words and told of his refusal to take his psychiatric medication and his denial that anything was wrong with him. I did not mention the pizza episode. The hearing lasted fifteen minutes, and the judge committed Kermit to a seventy-two-hour psychiatric hold, which meant that the hospital could now forcibly treat him.

When Kermit returned to the ward, he was thoroughly pissed. He began to throw things around—the emesis basin, tape, gauze, trauma shears, the water pitcher—and then he started pulling everything off his bed. The ward clerk called a Code 5 overhead, and the security guards and big male nurses came scrambling in to pin Kermit to the bed while he screamed, "FUCK YOU! I WILL KILL ALL OF YOU!"

A nurse pushed Valium through his IV until Kermit's body began to shudder and relax. Forty-five minutes later, while he was still dozing, a crew came to take him to his new lodgings on the psychiatric ward. As I watched him go down the hall and out of sight, it occurred to me that I should probably try to feel some pathos or remorse for him, but instead, I felt relieved: he was off my service and not my problem anymore. I went back to my office and paged Fleet, to tell him that Kermit's infection was clearing, that the court had detained him, and he was on his way to the psychiatric ward.

Fleet said, "You got to keep close tabs on that guy. I'll stop by to see him tomorrow."

Sequel

The following week, the chief of medicine, who happened to be an oncologist, called to say that she wanted a patient of hers admitted for chemotherapy. The patient had a treatable form of lymphoma. I wrote down the medical record number and pulled up his electronic chart. His name was Bill Justice, and he was a repeat customer.

Bill checked in at the cancer clinic and then walked over to Four, where a bed awaited him. He was a thin redheaded man. When I came to meet him, he was sitting in bed, watching television. We shook hands. He seemed familiar, and as we talked, I realized he was a writer at one of the newsweeklies.

"Wow," he said. "Wow. You're a doctor? But you're, like, my age."

I told him I'd take care of him while he was in the hospital, and then he'd return to see my boss for long-term care. I was not completely comfortable with the idea of having a well-known writer as a patient—it was not unlike taking care of a lawyer—but it was a three-day hospitalization, and the big decisions in this case would be made by the cancer specialists. He had discussed the chemotherapy plan thoroughly with his oncologist and knew he had a "good" form of cancer that could be cured. They were optimistic that the new drugs would work.

Before we could get started, though, he'd need a central line, through which the chemotherapy could be infused. Most patients getting chemo got a permanent line, which was more comfortable and posed less risk of infection, but Bill had been known to inject illicit drugs on occasion, so a permanent line wasn't an option.

I began to study his neck, to feel where the muscles came to a point just above his collarbone, and I found the pulse of his carotid artery. Bill told me that his jugular vein was pretty scarred and adherent to his neck muscles, owing to his habit of injecting there. But he'd depleted his veins everywhere else. I'd gotten some tough ones and was fairly confident I would get it in, so I began cleaning the skin. I draped a sterile cloth over his face, and he said, "I heard that if you inject into a line just once, it can kill you."

"What you inject goes straight to your heart."

"I know a guy who had a—pick line? He shot cocaine, and half of his body became paralyzed instantly. Have you ever heard of that?"

I hadn't, but I told him that people didn't leave the hospital with a central line because of significant health risks. There was a remote chance the paralysis story was true; maybe the line hadn't been used in a while, and when the addict shot up, he dislodged clotted blood that sailed through a window in his heart and on up to his brain, causing a stroke.

"He can't walk anymore," Bill said.

"I guess that can happen," I said.

"Wow."

"I promise we will pull out the line and stop chemotherapy if you do that."

Bill said, "I'm not stupid. I got to beat this cancer."

Afterward I headed downstairs to Marv Hooley's room. Marv was having another fever and the nurse wanted to know if I wanted more blood cultures, since he'd had a number of them and nothing had turned up. His oxygen level was still low; I pulled over at a computer and clicked on a chest X-ray done earlier in the day. Fluid surrounded his right lung. It was probably related to his heart failure, but what if it wasn't? He didn't come to clinic regularly, and this might be the only chance to make the diagnosis, to get him pointed toward appropriate therapy.

Marv was reading the newspaper when I got to his room. He looked freshly showered, and he had an oversize hair pick planted in his afro. My pager went off. I decided to ignore it for a minute.

"I feel pretty good," Marv said. I told him I was worried about the fever, that I'd like to remove some of the lung fluid and send it to the laboratory for analysis.

"You do what you need to do," he said. I returned with a permission slip for him to sign and laid out supplies on the bedside table.

He said, "I had bad sweats last night." I nodded. My mind chanted the possibilities: hidden infection, tuberculosis, blood clot, cancer. I numbed his skin and got into a pocket of fluid an inch below the surface. It drew easily into the syringe, the color of rubies. I pressed my lips together.

"Now that feels better," Marv said. "Thank you. That didn't hurt a bit. You all are taking such good care of me."

The fluid analysis showed a high lymphocyte count which, alongside the sweats and weight loss suggested tuberculosis. I tracked down the charge nurse on Three.

"Are you kidding?" She reached into her back pocket for a list of patients on the wards. First order of business was to bump someone from one of the three private rooms, move Marv in, and turn on the ventilation system, which filtered out anything potentially contagious in his room. As soon as he was settled, I geared up in a full space helmet with air filter and went in. "I assume you heard," I said, raising my voice over the buzz of the filter. Hopefully he could read lips.

"Tuberculosis," he said. He made a clucking noise. He was standing at the mirror, combing his hair, which stood straight out from his head in a globe-shaped mass.

"We'll run a couple more tests to find out if you're infectious." If this were the case, the hospital would have to test the several patients and dozens of staff who'd been exposed to him, would have to offer preventive treatment to those whose tests turned positive.

"That's all right."

"Hopefully we can get you out of isolation soon."

"You all are doing the best you can," he said. He seemed in no hurry to move along.

The next morning there was a bunch of new business for me to attend to. There was a woman from Cleveland with heart failure who, for reasons unknown, spent her summers at the YWCA shelter in downtown Seattle. There was an elderly man who broke his hip and was here for a repair; in the meantime he needed some assistance with his heart arrhythmia. I had to hustle through rounds because there was a noontime faculty meeting, so I blew through my visit with the purple-haired HIV patient. Only as I was walking out of the room did it occur to me that he was not getting better because he didn't have an infection—he had heart failure. I headed back in to ask a few more questions, to talk about what was probably going on.

"That makes total sense, man," he said. "I just don't feel like I have pneumonia."

Then I was back on my feet and finishing my circumnavigation of the ward, and on into the workrooms in the core to crank out notes for the charts.

At the medical staff meeting there was lunch in the back of the room: lentil soup and a green salad obscured by a pile of shredded cheese. About fifty people were seated when I arrived, mostly internists and surgeons, some of whom were quite well known. I recalled that some of the doctors had been my attendings five and six years ago, when I was a medical student.

A few minutes after the hour, a tall man with funky glasses stood and called a quorum. The printed agenda identified him as medical director Dr. Scott Barnhart, and I studied him curiously. He wore a light blue silk tie, and his shirt-sleeves were rolled up, as though he'd just come from performing a bronchoscopy in the ICU. He also had the build of a former college football player. He thanked everyone for coming and started the meeting by saying, "Dictations are killing us."

I glanced at the agenda I was clutching and saw that the first item was the electronic medical-record system that was to be unrolled over the next two years. *How fascinating*, I thought, reaching for my pager to see if I had missed any calls earlier. I hadn't, so I wondered how long I would need to stay, feigning interest, before I could get up and leave.

But Scott's voice surprised me: he sounded kind and patient, like the sort of doctor who implored you to please call him by his first name. He began his pitch with the facts: transcriptionists charged the hospital between $20 and $40 for every dictated note, he said. The lengthy ones that the medicine residents often performed were particularly expensive, which meant that for unsponsored patients—a euphemism for patients without health insurance—the hospital was paying tens of thousands of dollars yearly just to keep records of their visits.

The solution he proposed was draconian: doctors would have to start typing their own notes. "I don't see that we have another choice," he said. A predictable murmuring erupted in the crowd, and Scott hastened to add that he was using the electronic application himself when he attended on the wards. He admitted it was time-consuming up front.

"I'm not a very good typist," he noted. He tried to sell the idea that it would eventually save everybody some time, and that it would facilitate billing.

A nurse practitioner from the HIV clinic asked, "Would you recommend typing lessons? Because I'm typing my notes and it takes me three or four hours per day. I finish after my son is in bed. If we really lose money every time we see a patient, maybe we should see fewer patients."

Scott shifted from foot to foot. Seeing fewer uninsured patients was what private practitioners did; it was a practice that, at least in theory, ran contrary to the hospital's mission.

Finally he said, "How many patients you see is up to your clinic director."

Dr. Nancy Sugg, who ran the Pioneer Square medical clinic for the homeless, raised her hand. She wore a knee-length skirt and flats.

"I'm a clinic director," she said. "Should we limit the number of appointments so people can type their notes?"

Scott said, "Something to consider is that *we're* paying when we see many of our patients."

Mercifully, my pager rang. I'd made an adequate show of professional citizenship, I decided, and jumped at the chance to duck out. The page was from Alice Brownstein, in the ED, who wanted me to come admit a woman named Claudia O'Donnell. She was perched at the edge of a gurney, puffing away at thirty times per minute when I arrived a few moments later. She suffered from a chronic lung disorder called bronchiectasis, which in some patients caused frequent bouts of pneumonia. I introduced myself and said I would be admitting her to the hospital. She rolled her eyes back into her head and wailed, "Noooo!"

I pointed out that she was receiving four liters of oxygen, that her oxygen level was marginal, and that her chest X-ray showed pneumonia in two of the lobes of her lungs. Standard medical care for this diagnosis was intravenous antibiotics, and for me to send her home would be malpractice, I said. She started to hyperventilate and clutch at her throat. She began wheezing audibly, then took a deep, controlled breath.

"My fingers are numb," she said, and laughed nervously.

"Help me understand why you don't want to be hospitalized," I said.

"Last night I thought I was going to die." She paused in between her deep breaths. "I've never called 9-1-1 before. If I go home right now—I don't know. I'm afraid of that. But I don't have health insurance. I can't afford to be here."

She was self-employed and worked as a personal chef, so she could be more selective about the clients and hours she took on. One of her clients was a doctor who had recently provided her with a week's worth of antibiotics, in hopes that her condition would turn around. She told me she knew it wasn't the ideal way to go about things, but she felt she should give it a shot. When her condition still didn't improve, she had attempted to make an appointment with her nurse practitioner, who worked at a community health clinic, but hadn't been able to get in quickly enough.

At least Claudia had a primary care provider, I thought. She was lucky to live close to a community health clinic that provided great medical care, and which charged patients on a sliding scale. Claudia said she trusted her provider, who had urged had her several times to get linked in with a lung specialist.

"She says she's in over her head with me," Claudia said, but she seemed fine with the fact that her nurse practitioner was not a leading bronchiectasis expert, and thrilled to be able to get medical care without doing major damage to her bank account.

Had Claudia seen a specialist, it was possible that she wouldn't have gotten so sick, but it also probably wouldn't have saved her any money, nor prevented the hospitalization. The choices she made weren't for lack of understanding of how serious her disease was, I knew; her older brother had died from the same condition four years back, and her father had died from it thirty years earlier.

Instead, she had been gambling on a spontaneous recovery, just like the millions of other uninsured patients in America who bet against their health, who delayed preventive care and health maintenance services because of upfront costs. Now she was on the losing side of the bet and puffing away in the Harborview ED. She seemed scared, and she seemed stuck. In a month, she would be the age her brother had been when he'd died, and there were limited prospects for her to get commercial health insurance. I wondered how long she would remain healthy enough to work.

Claudia was typical of many of the uninsured patients I'd met at Harborview, most of whom were working very hard just to get by. Claudia herself was self-reliant and entrepreneurial; the problem was that she worked for herself. In fact, about three-quarters of the 46 million uninsured and 16 million underinsured in the United States were working adults like Claudia; many had low-paying jobs, and in Washington State, a significant number had become uninsured when the state's Basic Health program dropped their coverage, due to shrinking legislative funding.

The health care system was a bad deal no matter how you sliced it for the 62 million people—or one-fifth of the U.S. population—that had diminished access to health care, which included anyone with inadequate, episodic, or no insurance. Those with no insurance paid out of pocket for all of their medical care, and when patients paid out of pocket, they were typically charged sticker price. What was particularly galling about the pricing system, if you counted yourself among the uninsured, was that insurance companies and government agencies received deep discounts on account of their purchasing power. An insurance company, for example, might pay between $54 and $77 for the chest X-ray Claudia had gotten in the emergency department—and Medicaid might pay $40—but she personally would likely be liable for the full $121. And then there was the problem that sticker prices were always on the rise, since this was one way for hospitals to recoup the deep discounts.

Washington State had passed a law requiring hospitals to charge patients on a sliding scale according to their income. Only those who earned at least three times the federal poverty limit would have to pay the full price of medical care.

For Claudia, a single person with no dependents, three times the poverty level was $31,464 per year, which provided some cushion. Should she require a week's hospitalization, though, the bill could still wipe out a significant chunk of her income.

I assured Claudia that I would have the financial counseling folks come talk with her. The hospital was good about working with patients to get the bills settled, I said. Like most patients to whom I pitched this idea, though, Claudia did not look reassured, and the truth was that I didn't really know what the financial counselors could do for her, what fraction of the bill they would ask her to pay. It occurred to me that whatever charitable deduction the hospital might provide for Claudia would just come out of what another patient paid. The whole system seemed very unfair to her: the insurance companies were charged the least—though they paid the bills most reliably—while those who lacked insurance but made too much for government insurance often received a whopping bill. To tangle matters further, I (like most clinicians) had very little idea what a bag of IV fluid cost, or a course of the antibiotic piperacillin-tazobactam, or a chest CT, which Claudia would need during her stay. I wondered if I did know the price of every medication and therapy, whether I would withhold standard care because of how much it would cost the patient.

"So I'm going to write admitting orders?" I confirmed.

"What can I do?" she shrugged. "Maybe you can send me home tomorrow."

"That would depend on whether you feel better. Don't you think?"

Claudia sighed and didn't answer.

M arv's test results were waiting upstairs when I finally returned to the ward, and he was making his bed when I came into his room sans space suit.

"I know how busy it gets for the nurse," he said, tucking his sheets under the mattress.

"I have some news for you," I said. "You're not infectious." The sputum samples showed that he was not coughing up tuberculosis, that the disease was confined to the fluid around the lungs.

"Thank god!" he said. He seemed genuinely relieved.

"You'll have to take antibiotics for nine months. You can't drink alcohol while you're taking these antibiotics, because the combination can damage the liver."

"I'm done drinking!" he said.

"You'll need a water pill for your heart."

"That's fine!"

"And how will you quit drinking?"

"I'm done. I quit."

"Do you want to do AA? I can ask the social worker to bring a list of AA groups and treatment centers."

"That would be good."

I said, "What would really help you is a regular doctor."

"I will do whatever you tell me to," he said.

B y the end of the week the service had become busy enough that I didn't notice it when Bill Justice disappeared. The first I heard of it was when a nurse paged to say that he had disconnected his IV and seemed to be gone, and she reminded me that he still had his central line. *The bastard*, I thought. I went for his whole story about his paralyzed friend. I was angry because of the conundrum he presented: if I refused him a line, he couldn't get chemotherapy. If I placed the line, he had an instant way to get high—and to overdose.

By the time Bill returned, somnolent, I was purple in the face. I strode into his room with his nurse and said, "I thought we discussed how you weren't supposed to leave the hospital."

"I went down for a smoke," he said. He could barely keep his eyes open.

"Four hours is pretty long for a smoke." I signaled to the nurse, who pushed a dose of naloxone into his line, a drug that reversed opiates such as heroin. About fifteen seconds later, Bill was sitting up, wide awake.

"What happened?"

"You got Narcan."

"What?"

"It's a drug that reverses the effect of opiates."

He started to look mad.

"We had a deal," I said, pulling on gloves and tearing open a package of gauze. I snipped the stitches around his line, told him to breathe in deeply and then breathe out. I pulled the line in a brisk movement.

"What did you just do?" he said.

"You've finished your course of chemotherapy. We'll check your labs in the morning, make sure the electrolytes look normal, make sure your counts are OK, and then you can get out of here."

"I didn't use anything!" he exclaimed.

"Do you want to prove it?"

"Sure."

I handed him a urine specimen cup.

"Okay, all right," he said, turning up his palms.

"I'm going to send you to see your oncologist in clinic next week. If she wants to give you the chemotherapy personally, and tie you to the recliner in the infusion unit, she can do it."

"Wow," Bill said. "Wow. That was really stupid of me."

"Yeah. The discharge paperwork will be ready first thing in the morning. If you need a ride, Barb will be happy to arrange one for you."

Later, when I typed up a summary of his hospitalization, I realized I probably didn't have a lot of sympathy for him because I thought I knew where he came from. He was an educated person, with opportunities that most of the patients never had. Maybe I couldn't sympathize because I knew he was relatively well-to-do, because I knew he had all the tools he needed to get his act together. Maybe I saw his drug addiction less as a disease and more as a personal failure. This wasn't the same standard I applied to other patients. I was furious because we were providing his cancer treatment free of charge, because the other hospital patients would pay for his care, and I was upset, more than anything else, that he was unappreciative. He had waited until receiving all of the chemotherapy to shoot up, so as to not jeopardize his treatment.

I realized that Bill wasn't too different from Dave French, the patient whose father had wanted to stop his life support because he was a drug user and a street person. Perhaps I was feeling a little of what Dave's father had felt a hundred times, having lived through decades of his son's lies, and dozens of drug relapses.

There was a distinction in my mind, though. Bill Justice's self-harm was the direct result of something I had done. Dave could have left the hospital and killed himself with drugs, but he would have to work harder at it.

By the time I was ready to sign out for the week, Claudia O'Donnell's bronchiectasis exacerbation had slowly started to come around, thankfully, since the only medications she had let me give her were intravenous antibiotics. She had refused to let me order a CT scan of her chest, which might have shown why she wasn't improving very quickly, and provided a basis for more aggressive therapy. If she left in a day, she would be liable for six days of hospitalization, at a base cost of $1,200 per night, and before I sat down to write my chart notes, I called financial counseling again to make sure they had received her paperwork.

But the rest of the news on the ward was bright. The patient with purple hair was feeling healthy again and had gone home. The elderly man with the hip fracture was headed for a rehab facility, where he would receive intensive physical therapy, and the woman from Cleveland was ready to get out of the hospital, at least until she ran out of medications and needed to be hospitalized again.

Barb said, "Where does she want to go?"

Sarcastically I said, "She wants to go back to Cleveland, and frankly she would be better served by her cardiologists there, since they've known her for years."

"Well, her Medicaid is through the state of Ohio. She can't file for Medicaid here unless she cancels her Ohio benefits."

This was a non sequitur to me, so I said, "She's been staying at the women's shelter. Maybe she can just go back there."

A couple of hours later, Barb handed the patient a printed bus ticket to Cleveland, along with snappy directions on how to get to the station forty-five minutes before the departure time.

"The ride will take two days and fourteen hours. Travel safely, and don't forget to get up and stretch your legs every now and then," she said. The patient looked bewildered, but the ticket was paid for, and she was going.

When I saw Barb a while later she said, "We had to dip into the special fund. It's cheaper than bringing her back into the hospital next time she gets sick."

"I thought you said she had Medicaid."

"She has Medicaid in Ohio," she replied. Medicaid was state-based, she told me, and only reimbursed care in the state where a patient was registered; it didn't matter where she was actually living. I thanked Barb several times, impressed by her power to move patients around, despite limited resources. The suggestion, moreover, was that medical care was as much about finding social solutions as it was about supplying health services.

It's on the Calendar

I was passing through a busy clinic waiting room when a stocky man squinted at my identification badge, made eye contact, and said, "You probably don't remember me, but my name is Dave French, and you saved my life." He reached out to shake my hand.

My first thought was that Dave was much taller than I had imagined. He wore a sport jacket over a cable-knit sweater, and his eyes seemed enlarged due to his thick glasses. I realized he was walking, talking, and making sense.

I got over my initial shock and said, "I remember taking care of you. You were pretty sick. You know, a lot of doctors took care of you."

"I don't know if you heard, but I've been clean of drugs for ten months, since the day I came to the hospital. It's the longest I've been sober since I was fourteen years old."

"You look good."

"I have some questions about what happened to me. The last thing I remember is the pavement coming up to my face," he said.

"I can try to answer your questions."

"I only remember a couple of things about being in the hospital. One is someone coming in my room and pointing at the garbage can and saying, 'You are like this! You are trash!'" He gestured emphatically at a garbage can in the corner of the waiting room. "I remember that the person who said this was a small Asian woman. Was that you?"

I smiled and said, "That wasn't me."

He shook his head. "I remember it so clearly, but I could have dreamed it. When you came walking through here, I was sure I recognized you."

"I spent a lot of time at the side of your bed, but you were comatose."

He told me about the excruciating pain in his legs and lifted his cane to show how he walked.

"We didn't know if you would wake up, let alone walk again," I said. I wondered how much he knew about his father's request to stop life support, but this wasn't the time or place to ask, and anyway, I had to get to the ED to hear about a couple of patients that Alice wanted to admit, then get to a financial meeting with Administration. "Maybe we can get coffee sometime, and I'll try to answer your questions about what happened."

Dave told me he was staying at his sister's rural home a couple hours east of Seattle, that he had lost his driver's license and didn't have a car anymore. I scribbled down his telephone number and promised to call.

"Boy, I'm real glad to finally meet you," he said.

In the Fishbowl, I learned from Alice that four new patients were coming to my service: a drug user with an abscess, a nice young woman with an infected kidney, a construction worker who was suffering from intestinal bleeding, and a man named Paul Brown, whom she had saved for last.

I groaned.

"So sorry," she said. "But he was asking for you. He says you understand him."

Paul was a thirty-seven-year-old who was shot in the stomach a decade ago, survived a ten-hour operation, and now was missing his spleen, his right kidney, and twenty-eight of the thirty feet of his intestinal tract, which meant that when Paul ate a cheeseburger, the thing passed through him practically intact. He got his nutrition intravenously—a gallon bag of yellow liquid protein and carbs, plus a small bottle of fats—every night.

I'd taken care of him twice in the last couple of months, and he was back at the county hospital with the same problem again: a bloodstream infection. All of the infectious disease doctors believed he was deliberately contaminating the line because the resulting infection usually required hospitalization. The issue of the moment, however, was that Paul's IV was ready to blow and he urgently needed a central line for pain meds and nutrition.

I trekked up to the eighth floor, where he was killing time watching TV in bed.

"Howdy. How do you feel?"

"Well, the pain is out of control. It's an 11." He was referencing the 1-to-10 rating scale for pain, with 1 indicating no pain and 10 equivalent to the pain of childbirth. The translation was that I'd have to pump him full of narcotics so he'd cooperate with the plan.

"Where does it hurt?" I thought of what I had heard Fleet say: *Is the pain focal, or is it cosmic?*

"Around the port," Paul said. He reclined comfortably on his pillow. During his previous hospitalization he had described pain at this same spot, where the intravenous nutrition plugged into his chest.

I put on gloves and unbuttoned the gown at his shoulder. "How long has it hurt?"

"It always hurts." He grinned crookedly. The port looked a little swollen, though not terrible, and before I could touch the area he screamed. I told him I'd need to put in a central line.

"You better knock me out to do it," he said. He seemed delighted by the idea.

"Fine."

I gathered up supplies and asked the nurse to push a milligram of Dilaudid. As I was setting up, Paul said, "One won't cut it. I'm telling you, I need at least four."

I looked at the nurse and said, "Fine, let's start with two and we'll have two more ready." She pushed the meds. I set up the supplies and scrubbed his skin. By the time I was ready to inject the local anesthetic, he was a little dopey from the pain meds.

"Shit!" he screamed as the anesthetic went into his skin. "I'm not kidding you—two isn't going to cut it!"

I wanted to roll my eyes, but instead I told the nurse to push the rest of the Dilaudid. As the medicine went in, Paul sighed.

"Now we're talking," he said.

I placed the sterile drape over him, letting it fall over his face so I didn't have to watch his theatrics. The line itself was a cinch; I hit the vein on the first pass, and the rest of the procedure took about ten minutes more.

"Mr. Brown, the line is in. I just need to sew it into place."

No response. I lifted the drape and an exhalation whistled out of his nose. He remained zonked as I sewed two stitches into his skin and tied my knots, looping and pulling, under then over.

"We're all finished," I said. I pulled the drape off him and admired the clean job I'd done, then shook his shoulder. His eyes fluttered, he took a deep snorting breath, and I shook my head.

At the nursing station I wrote a quick note about the central line, about how readily the needle entered the vein, about how the blood flowed smoothly through each of the three lines when I checked its functioning.

I flipped to the back section of the chart and wrote an order for Dilaudid every few hours, intravenous Benadryl for itching, and ibuprofen to be given around the clock. During our afternoon conversation, he'd tell me that ibuprofen was a waste of his time, that it didn't do anything for him. I'd tell him that unlike narcotics, which only cover up pain, ibuprofen actually healed inflammation, and that I wanted him to take both. Prescribing ibuprofen helped me feel that I was doing something besides feeding his drug habit, anyway.

I was just two floors away from my scheduled meeting with the hospital administrators, and I needed to get moving, so I washed my hands, buttoned my white coat, and headed upstairs. I'd never had so many meetings: faculty meetings, staff meetings, mentoring huddles, team strategy sessions, section meetings, billing reviews—none of which really seemed to pertain to the care of live patients. Apparently this was how things worked in the real world, and I'd resigned myself to it. I entered a top-floor conference room and a man and a woman rose to shake my hand. My colleague had already arrived. The topic: first-quarter review.

The man said, "Thank you for coming. We hear that you're busy."

"We're getting crushed, but thank you for asking," I said, sinking into a plush chair.

The man said cheerfully, "We don't need to make this long, so let's just get started with your first set of numbers." *Click.* Our heads swiveled toward the first slide, which glowed a bright green.

"Every time you see a patient, you get a little bit of credit, which we call a Relative Value Unit. For example, we assign 1.64 RVUs the first time you see a patient with a skin infection and, for example, 1.32 RVUs for any subsequent visit with a patient who has heart failure and diabetes." The administrators looked quite pleased with the RVUs.

"The hospital wants you to hit 180 RVUs a month. That's standard in the university setting. Of course, targets in the private world are considerably higher, but we're a public hospital, we have inefficiencies like our residency programs and such, so to be fair we adjust the RVU level downward.

"Let's review monthly RVU totals to date," he said. *Click.* A graph materialized, showing our team averaging 30, 69, and 95 RVUs in the first three months of work. My colleague and I exchanged glances. September, at 95 RVUs, had been numbingly busy.

My colleague said, "We got killed in September, and our RVUs are half of where you want them."

No one was smiling. "That's right," the man said.

"We would need to see thirty hospital patients per day."

"I can't remember patients' names when there are fifteen, let alone what's wrong with them," I said. My pager rang.

"Do you need to get that?" the woman said.

"I can wait until we're done."

"These are the RVU numbers that Scott Barnhart feels comfortable with."

"People make these numbers without getting sued?"

"We really can't speak to that side of it, the Risk Management side. We're just here to talk about the RVU expectations," the woman said.

Click. "Let's look at collections," the man said. The hospital received about $45,000 for services in the first quarter; our salaries, benefits, and office space cost double that figure.

"Harborview takes in about twenty-seven cents on the dollar," the woman said. "Of course, you're seeing indigents who are never going to pay their bill, and we know that. The hospital does write off charity care." She did not mention the huge dent that insurance company discounts made in the collection rate.

But the numbers were not making sense, so I asked, "Can you help me understand? Because the way I read this, we took in $60,000."

"That's the amount before the dean's taxes. The dean's office takes a percentage, then the Department of Medicine takes a percentage. What's left over comes back to the hospital."

"So the hospital is really collecting seventeen or eighteen cents on the dollar."

"It's complicated," the woman said.

The man said, "The bottom line is that you need to increase RVUs to meet the hospital's goals." My pager rang again; the woman betrayed a hint of annoyance and decided that the meeting was over.

"I'm so pleased that we were able to meet today," the man said, extending his hand. "We'll be in touch."

The pages were from a resident who wanted me to know that Mirabelle Fleming, the young woman with pulmonary hypertension, had arrived at the hospital intubated and was breathing by a mechanical ventilator at the very highest settings. She had cocaine and heroin in her urine, the resident said, and probably wouldn't survive the night.

"I guess she wants everything done. I saw your last note."

"That's what she told us."

I walked downstairs to Two. She was so puffy that her eyes were just slits, and three nurses were hovering around her bed, getting ready to flip her onto her stomach. This last-ditch effort to prolong her life made me think of something I heard occasionally during my training: *we're just rearranging deck chairs on the* Titanic. The following day, when I remembered to check the ICU record, I saw that her name had been removed from the bed list. The resident told me that they ran a slow code, meaning they went through the motions of resuscitation without hope that she would come back, and "declared" her after the first round of drugs and shocks failed.

I filled Barb in at rounds, and she clucked and said, "Kid, remember that she had an addiction, and she made some bad choices."

I was beginning to appreciate how unusual Dave French's recovery and sobriety were. I had learned what happened to him from the critical care physicians. He came off the ventilator after two weeks, started to talk, relearned to eat regular food, and suffered a brief bout of pneumonia. He didn't need kidney dialysis anymore. A CT scan showed that his lungs were full of blood clots, which had probably caused his sudden collapse. The clots probably came from impurities in injected drugs, I found out, and this became the first of my concessions to Sam, who'd blamed Dave's critical illness on his drug use. Dave had left the hospital in a wheelchair, one month after he'd first been hospitalized. He was headed for a rehabilitation facility, where the plan was for him to begin walking again.

Some weeks later, Dave did something that a number of our patients failed to do: he returned for a checkup. Randy Curtis, a critical care physician and end-of-life specialist, had accepted him as a patient. Curtis had performed the usual pulmonologist tasks, such as asking about his chronic cough and ordering tests of lung volume and function, and had sent Dave's sputum to the laboratory for analysis.

Curtis had also discovered that Dave knew about Sam's request to stop life support. Dave said he didn't fault his father, and he himself still felt uncertain about whether he should have been kept alive. Curtis asked him what he wanted if he relapsed into drug use again and became ill enough to require life support. Did he want to be resuscitated? Who should make the decisions if he was unresponsive? Dave mentioned his brother or father as possibilities, but said that he'd like to give the matter some thought first.

He arrived early for his next appointment and spent most of the visit talking about his father Sam's new heart-failure diagnosis, which carried a prognosis of less than one year to live. He told Curtis that his father had beaten cancer fifteen years earlier, and he had always seen his father as invincible. He was having a hard time not being able to choose him as his power of attorney. Curtis pressed Dave to make his decision by the following appointment.

On Dave's third visit, five months after his hospitalization, he walked into clinic for the first time, leaning on a cane. He could go up to three city blocks before leg pain incapacitated him or he ran out of breath. He was attending Narcotics Anonymous meetings on Mondays and Thursdays and called the group his lifeline. He told Curtis that before his illness, he thought that drugs provided the ultimate high, and now he believed that one use would kill him. He wanted to volunteer in the emergency room so he could remind himself what would happen if he touched drugs again. Curtis encouraged him to do so.

Dave said he'd chosen his sister Diana as power of attorney. He had described his last wishes to her in detail, which included mechanical ventilation and other forms of life support if there was a reasonable chance of regaining his current health. He did not want to be in the ICU longer than one month, he said, and he did not want life support again if he had started using drugs. He believed that if he was using, the drugs would kill him one way or another, and he should just be let go. When I heard this, I assumed that Sam had planted the idea; only later, after I'd become acquainted with Dave, did he convince me that the idea originated with him.

Not long afterward, I stopped in to ask Curtis a few questions about Dave. The bread and butter of Curtis's clinical practice was in advising other doctors and patients' families to let patients go gently and gracefully, without deploying every advanced bit of medical technology. Right off the bat, Curtis endorsed Sam's point of view: the most likely outcome for Dave was still that he would return to street life, and one day a drug overdose would finish him off. Curtis had seen this happen hundreds of times with Harborview patients. It was incredibly rare for a shooter to turn clean, he said, even after a catastrophic illness such as this one.

We chatted for a while about the particulars of the case. I mentioned that Dave had been in severe septic shock on the night he arrived, and that to keep him going we'd given him three vasopressor medications at maximum doses. Curtis suggested that I tabulate Dave's APACHE score, which researchers used to rate the severity of a patient's illness, to see what his odds of survival had been at the outset. Perhaps the most important consideration, he said, was Dave's quality of life in the aftermath of his ICU stay. He made particular mention of the fact that patients with prolonged ICU stays often live with disabling pain, and Dave had been no exception. His leg pains hadn't improved much in the three visits he'd made to clinic, and Curtis now suggested that this could have been adequate justification to stop life support in the ICU. It interested me that Curtis still felt there were legitimate medical reasons that justified withholding aggressive care during Dave's first days in the ICU. It didn't matter that he'd survived.

After our conversation, I logged on to a computer in the ICU. The APACHE score for Dave's first night of hospitalization gave him a 93 percent chance of dying. I stood with my arms crossed, coming to terms with the idea that the odds against him had been phenomenal from the start and that his recovery and persistent sobriety were so unusual that I might not see such a thing again in my career.

All the same, I was thrilled. I was thrilled that Dave was grappling with difficult decisions, that he'd decided his actions should have consequences. It interested me that he saw his drug use as something akin to a terminal cancer that could resurface at any time, that he'd put the highest stakes on a drug relapse and told his family and his doctors to let him go if he used drugs even once. It seemed that he was trying to make good on the new and unexpected life that he'd gained. I was only sad that his father was sick and probably wouldn't live to enjoy his sobriety, if it lasted. *Maybe this will bolster Dave's resolve*, I thought. Maybe he would decide to stay sober because there was not much time left to show his formidable father what he was made of.

A rare bug called rhodococcus was growing from the blood of Paul Brown—the patient with two feet of intestine—and a CT scan of his lungs showed a spray of irregular nodules that were probably little balls of infection. The nodules were new since the previous CT scan, done a couple of months earlier.

"It's probably nothing," the infectious disease (ID) fellow said. "But I would resend blood cultures, and try to get tissue." The lung spots were possibly a fungal infection owing to his long-term intravenous nutrition.

In the afternoon I headed up to Eight to discuss the situation with Paul. He made a childish face and said, "Fungus?"

"I know, it's gross."

"Yeah, it's gross!" he said, but he was laughing. "Fungus among us." Paul didn't laugh a lot.

"We may have to take a piece of one of those to find out what it is."

Paul recoiled. "Does that involve a needle?"

"That would involve a needle at the least."

"Let me think about that one."

"It's possible we'll get an answer from the blood cultures."

"I like that idea."

"ID thinks the spots are probably related to the port."

"ID always thinks that," he said. I smiled, and then my pager rang.

"Okay, you gotta go," he said.

"I'll let you know what I hear. In the meantime, we'll continue with the antibiotics." I turned to leave.

He called after me: "Thanks for stopping by!"

As I headed downstairs again, I realized that Paul probably had an idea of what we said about him in the hallways, had the sense that he was judged. He lived with his mother, and I wondered what his home life was like, why he seemed to enjoy the hospital so much.

The pathologist called me to report on Paul Brown's lung biopsy: "It's all nonspecific granulomata," she said. "I combed through every slice." Nothing was growing from the new blood cultures, so if there had been an infection, it seemed to have cleared with antibiotics. The spots on his lungs were destined to remain a mystery, perhaps forever. I went upstairs to tell Paul the results and discharge him home. He had been in-house for five days, considerably fewer than usual. I doubted that the antibiotics, which he always got, were responsible; it was probably the pain meds that really helped him.

Paul said, "Not that I want more tests, but don't we need to figure out what these things are on my lungs?"

"Well, we care whether the spots are an infection or cancer, right? And the biopsy says that they're neither. So they may be a reaction to your intravenous nutrition. They don't seem to be anything to worry about." Paul made another face.

I pulled up a chair. "We got good news, right? You don't have cancer. But we didn't think you had cancer, because the spots came on really fast. Cancer doesn't usually do that. We thought you might have an infection, but you don't, according to the cultures. It could be a weird bug that takes a few weeks to grow, but I think that's unlikely, and anyway, there's nothing we can do about that right now. We just have to wait. Does that make sense?"

"Okay."

"I wish we understood why you get so many infections."

"It started with that first surgery," he said. "I came back eight times. They could never figure out why."

"Is your water on a well?

"No, I'm on city water. Why?"

"Just wondering, I guess, if it's something at home."

Paul gave me a searching, uninterpretable look. "I don't think so."

I stood. "I'll do the paperwork. You can get out of here sometime this afternoon."

"Can I get some pain medication to go?"

I sighed and said, "Sure."

Becoming Copass

O n an October evening, Michael Copass called the paramedics from home and said, "Boys, I need a ride." Minutes later, two of the Seattle medics he had selected and trained personally appeared at the end of his driveway, packed him into their rig, and rushed him to the hospital, where he was treated for a heart attack. He recuperated for a number of weeks before resuming a work schedule approved by his cardiologist.

Soon enough, though, he was back in the spin of hospital traffic, enforcing the commandments, his belt filled with pagers and cell phones. When he finally invited applications for an apprentice, Alice Brownstein thought, *Nobody can do this job.* Alice believed that Copass was a true hero because of the thousands of lives he had saved, and she also believed he was irreplaceable. He had worked almost every day for thirty years, arriving early in the morning and sometimes staying until after midnight. She would not survive the life he had lived, she told me over breakfast one morning. Still, she said, she felt a strong loyalty to Copass, who had attended her marriage to a veteran city paramedic. She knew that Copass considered the ED a family business, and she knew he wanted to groom his successor personally.

When we finished eating, Alice fortified herself with a latte, then headed for her next shift in the ED.

As time passed and no applicants emerged, Alice and four other ED attendings began to talk about a coalition to take on Copass's role—a junta, as some people called the fivesome. At first she was hesitant, since her husband wasn't crazy about her becoming his supervisor. She could understand his point of view. She liked when their shifts overlapped, enjoyed taking patients that he'd stabilized, and was grateful that he understood the pressures of her work. She wouldn't want him supervising her, either. But in time they both recognized that it was important for her to help Copass carry on his mission, and so she would refrain from interacting with the paramedics. For her husband's part, he would find a way to cope.

Some months later, the junta was hired on as Copass's deputies. Months before the start date, the group began to meet, sometimes carrying on late into the evening, and sometimes Copass came to lecture about the founding of the paramedic and airlift programs, about the history of resuscitation research, and about voter initiatives to support emergency services. It was as though the junta's first task was to form a collective memory about Harborview's modern era. Soon the group had hashed out five separate administrative domains: one person was responsible for learning about the airlift service, another for the paramedics, a third for medical education, and a fourth for quality improvement. Alice took on the fifth role of interfacing with the hospital, and they would each take turns as the emergency communications contact, available by phone twenty-four hours a day.

The junta was ready to launch in early summer. Alice's days began at 6 a.m., when she swallowed a latte and then joined morning rounds in the department with Copass and the residents. After rounds, she checked the hospital's census report, which was waiting in her email inbox. On an average Tuesday morning in September, she might find the house at 95 percent occupancy, with eighteen free beds on the wards, thirty-five likely to be empty by lunchtime, and sixteen scheduled admits, which were patients coming in for complex surgeries that had been months in the works. The census numbers gave a sense of what capacity there was in the hospital, gave some idea about whether the ED could admit patients freely that day, or if alternate measures would be required.

Hospital capacity depended upon a number of factors, such as the expedited evaluation and treatment of patients, on the patients' timely recoveries, on clinics that could see discharged patients in three or five days. Maintaining capacity required that when the president of the United States was in town raising money, as he had been during the most recent campaign season, one ED gurney would be saved for him as long as he was on the ground, but that his gurney would share space in the resuscitation suite with three trauma patients actively receiving care, and be turned over to an incoming patient the moment his jet lifted off. Copass had hammered into them that capacity was critical, that capacity was the only way to keep the doors open to the hospital's mission populations, which included those suffering from traumatic injury and burns, as well as the indigent and uninsured, many of whom had never received medical care anywhere except Harborview.

But capacity was in short supply that summer, and most mornings when Alice logged on to email, she learned that there was gridlock everywhere. On one particular Thursday morning in mid-July, at the height of trauma season, the morning email showed a grand total of minus-five beds, which meant that the two observation units were full and ED patients were resting in the back resuscitation suites, waiting for actual hospital beds to open up. After appraising the situation in the ED—two patients were headed to the OR and two more were awaiting hospital beds—Alice pushed off for the suites, to see if any of the patients were ready for discharge. She herself would send the emails and fill out the forms and cold-call the family members needed, so that a few more beds could be freed up.

Managing the ED could be a real challenge when hospital beds were jammed up. Sometimes there were just too many people who needed care at one moment: a stabbing victim who'd undergone an operative fix and was waiting in the recovery room for a general surgical bed; three patients in the ED who needed the OR within the hour, who would all require surgical beds sometime that day; and five new admits headed for the medicine floors with pneumonia or liver failure or heart attack. When the total number of beds was net negative and the ED was hopping, it was only a matter of time before the cell phone on Alice's hip rang, and she would know without checking the lighted display that it was Scott Barnhart calling.

A few minutes later, Alice and Scott convened at the Board, which was kept in a modest windowless office on the ground floor. The Board was an up-to-the-moment snapshot of every bed and patient at Harborview and generally served as the hospital's air traffic control center. The flow of traffic was managed by a verbally gifted nurse who was in constant contact with her colleagues on the floors above. This nurse was nearly always the first to know about ED patients needing hospitalization, about surgical cases being closed up, about improved ICU patients. She knew who was awaiting the OR and angiography suites, and she moved patients around the hospital in an elaborate game of musical chairs, trying to match four hundred unique individuals with the exact level of care required for that moment. ("I liked puzzles growing up," one of the air traffic control nurses told me. "I still do.")

The Board listed not only "real" hospital beds but also a number of beds that weren't technically affiliated with one of the wards—the negative beds, which still contained very real patients, and were often in the hinterlands of the ED. There could be as many negative beds as the hospital opted for, and at Copass's insistence, the hospital sometimes ran at thirty-five negative beds at a time, to keep traffic moving in the ED.

Scott had talked about closing the hospital doors at ten beds over capacity. In his view, a bed was not just somewhere to lie down and periodically receive some medical attention. A bed ought to guarantee high-quality medical care, and he believed it was hard to deliver consistent quality when patients were being housed in beds that doctors sometimes had difficulty locating. And anyway, the negative beds ought to be reserved for community emergencies, he believed.

Alice and Scott stood elbow to elbow studying the Board, and the day's outlook evolved as they watched. The phone rang, and after a moment the nurse at the desk said, "The patient wants his pain meds and wants to leave against medical advice? Is he competent? When can you get him the meds and get him out?" She hung up, located the patient's tag, and placed a red dot next to it, signalling a potential discharge. She had already chosen an ED patient to take the space being vacated, and now she moved the patient's tag into position. Alice noted that two more floor beds had opened since the 7 a.m. email update, and there was an open room in the cardiac ICU. In all, she predicted twenty-nine discharges. But it wasn't clear that twenty-nine open beds was enough to meet the hospital's needs that day.

Scott crossed his arms. He understood that Harborview could not come close to taking every patient that the other hospitals would rather not care for, and the question in his mind had become one of where the line should be drawn. Should the doors close at 95 percent capacity? At 105 percent capacity? The private hospitals in town often closed at 70 percent occupancy, because it was so expensive to maintain a nursing staff that could expand on very little notice. Scott did not believe that squeezing in every possible patient was the most effective way to care for sick people. Harborview's first priority was to operate safely, he felt.

The phone rang again, about an oxygen desaturation event on Three: a floor patient was probably going to need an ICU bed. The air traffic control nurse studied the board and said, "The two unit beds I have are going to ED patients. We'll probably have to do a straight swap with somebody being transferred out of ICU." She moved her finger down the ICU list, trying to determine who could be bumped.

Scott turned to Alice and said, "We're probably going to have to think about managing the front door. The attendings will need to decide which patients are appropriate for a Harborview bed." Alice knew that he was talking about "managing" admissions to the general medicine service. When a patient came to Harborview needing a surgical specialist, the patient received care without regard for how many open beds the hospital had, because Harborview was a referral center for these complicated cases. But general medicine patients could get standard medical care just about anywhere.

Alice frowned; she did not enjoy being the hospital's bouncer, didn't like telling her patients that they'd have to get additional care someplace else. Some patients simply refused, telling her that Harborview was the only hospital they trusted. Other patients agreed to a transfer, then waited in the ED for hours while she searched for an open bed and an accepting physician somewhere in the city. She found it especially frustrating when a patient she'd sent elsewhere reappeared in her ED days or weeks later, having been discharged without adequate medications or a follow-up appointment. These patients were often just as ill as they'd been before, and sometimes worse off, but they were generally too tired, out of breath, or in too much pain to express their disappointment about being shuffled around. Alice felt awful for these patients, who were often the homeless and addicted and chronically ill, the people who should feel they were regulars and deserved better treatment.

"Can we consider increasing discharges from the wards?" Alice said Scott. It seemed to her that they should be talking about improving the availability of hospital beds before the ED transported patients away.

Scott said that his office was in communication with the hospital's service chiefs and ward attendings, and the word was out that everybody needed to expedite the discharges. In fact, the administration had attempted many maneuvers in recent years to streamline hospital care. There was the staffing model that ensured the hospital had adequate nursing even when the census surged dramatically, which was pricey to maintain but was a crucial service for the hospital to offer. The level of physician manpower had been expanded significantly, and there were new operating rooms and patient care spaces in the works, which would add surge space. It took time to build an efficient hospital system, though, and to not just rely on stopgap solutions. Scott understood Alice's concern about closing the doors, but he believed the hospital needed to accept its limits.

A few minutes later Alice returned to the ED and studied the whiteboard. There were no pending admissions at the moment, but the situation could change, she knew. She turned and went into the radio room, where a computer screen reflected the bed status at eighteen other hospitals in the metropolitan area: most were tagged green, which meant the EDs were seeing patients and there were plenty of hospital beds in the city, in case Harborview needed to divert its ambulances for a little while. Still, Alice did not feel reassured. These were private hospitals, and her hunch was that most weren't terribly interested in patients that Harborview might deflect.

It was hard for Alice to imagine the hospital going on divert, which hadn't happened during the six years she'd worked there, first as a resident and then as an attending. The rumor was that the hospital hadn't closed its doors in thirty years, but Scott told me later that the hospital had in fact closed numerous times, briefly, during the 1990s. No one was officially keeping track.

Alice blew out of the radio room and went around the corner to the social work desk. The on-duty social worker told her the respite center on Maynard Street had some space for patients who needed nursing attention, and there was also the big downtown shelter, the DESC, that could place sick patients in infirmary bunks. Alice thought the respite center was a great choice for homeless people who needed a place to recuperate, but it usually filled by lunchtime, which left eighteen hours of the day in which patients would have to be discharged to either the shelter infirmary, which was routinely declined, or to no shelter at all. She scratched her head and thanked the social worker, then went into the Fishbowl to tell the ED attendings about the lack of capacity on the wards today, that there was preliminary talk about diverting the private ambulances.

Copass had worked harder than anybody else over the years to build Harborview's reputation for remaining open, for taking whoever came to the front door, and Alice knew that he would be upset by what was happening now. Nevertheless, she smiled and told the ED attendings that the respite facility and the DESC were still both good options at this point, and then she shut up. She felt that these morsels of information were plenty to keep attendings from hospitalizing patients who really just needed a place to stay warm for a couple of days, and she knew how difficult it could be to factor a small rationing decision on the hospital's behalf into the larger plan to address a patient's medical needs. What she didn't want, above all, was for a doctor to feel he had to send a moderately ill person out to the streets and hope for the best. That wasn't a very good way to practice medicine.

Before the morning ended, Alice glanced again at each of the half-dozen patients boarding in the ED, examining feet, listening to lungs, and checking oxygen levels. If she thought a patient was ready to go, she called the patient's primary doctor and shared her opinion as courteously as she could. If things remained gridlocked and she was feeling impatient, she would offer the hospital doctors help writing discharge orders. If the situation remained desperate, she'd walk upstairs to Three, select certain charts from the rack, and consider how to send those patients home too.

The radio clock showed 5:20 a.m. A Modest Mouse song came on. The sky outside was gray but bright, and Alice's brain swam. Was she supposed to get up and work, or was this an off day? Then she remembered: this was the second of five days that she was on as the ED communications person. She saw her pager sitting on the bedside table, groaned, then hoisted herself out of bed in one heroic movement.

Once she was up and moving about, she thought about the six beds that had been open when she left at dinnertime the previous evening. She was sure those beds had been filled and that the hospital would be saturated when she arrived in a half hour. She made herself aware of the fact that the temperature had hit the high 70s the previous afternoon, and the fact that her husband had never checked in last night—the paramedic shifts were twenty-four hours—which meant he'd been on the rig all night, ferrying sick people to the ED.

Fifteen minutes later she was pointed toward the hospital, trying to organize the morning in her head. She thought about which patients in the observation units could be discharged, and which attendings on the floors upstairs could be of use to her. In the radio room, Alice plugged in her laptop and checked the census email, which said:

Open beds: 0
ED boarders: 7
CCU: 0
ICU: 0
Floor: 0
Planned admits: 16

Copass entered the radio room and swiped a fistful of red grease pencils from a drawer beneath the counter. "It's a full house. Have all of the doctors gone away on summer vacation?"

Alice passed Copass the charts for rounds, and he set himself up at the counter, peeling a few shavings off each of the grease pencils as the residents filtered in. Rounds lasted about forty-five minutes, and afterward, Alice headed for the observation unit. She was on a land line prodding an intern through the discharge process when her cell phone rang.

Scott was staring at the Board with his arms crossed when Alice arrived, and the situation was ugly. Every bed in the house was spoken for, and there were now twelve patients waiting in the ED. The air traffic control nurse reviewed possible discharges: seven from the surgery floor, one from burns, eleven from medicine, a half dozen from ortho. She pulled the tags out as she talked.

"We've got hot weather through the weekend," Scott mused. He knew that the hospital needed to discharge as many patients as possible before the window of opportunity closed on Friday at 5 p.m., when many of the regular staff left for the weekend, and before people spent the weekend crashing their cars, drowning, getting stabbed or shot, and breaking major structural bones. Alice and Scott both knew that the hospital would have a hard time matching discharges to the weekend admissions.

Scott said, "It doesn't look good."

"We don't have much space in the ED," Alice said. "Observation is full, and we're boarding in the resuscitation suite."

"I still think divert is the way to go if things don't loosen up," Scott said. "You'll have to work on managing the front door again and see who doesn't absolutely need to be admitted."

"Which we are doing," Alice said. She did not like the idea of turning away ED patients when the hospital continued to bring in more than a dozen patients every day for planned, non-urgent surgeries. But planned admissions were a political hot potato at all of the Seattle hospitals, which did everything possible to preserve this group of patients and the revenue that they generated.

She left the huddle at the Board thinking about the prospect of the hospital going on divert. As long as she'd been around, the attitude had been that Harborview just didn't close. The house of Copass had been built by keeping the doors open, by taking on every patient who arrived needing care. If everybody needed to work harder, then that's what happened, she could hear Copass saying. Everyone was proud of how hard they worked. Alice wondered whether that attitude would change if the hospital went on divert.

By afternoon, in any case, discharges were beating admits by a good margin, and Alice was feeling optimistic again about the weekend. She went to the whiteboard in the ED and happily wrote her initials beside the name of a frequent flyer, Elaine Cook—a drinker who ended up in the ED every few days—and then put on a white coat and found the patient in the back resuscitation bay, where she was puffing away on a nebulizer.

"Hi Elaine," she said cheerfully. "What's happening?"

"Same fucking thing," Elaine answered. Her voice was guttural from smoking, like an old movie star. The standing protocol with Elaine was that she got two nebulizers plus a soda if she wanted one. Routine testing like blood work or yet another chest X-ray, or medication given for speculative reasons probably wouldn't make her better in the long run, and the unnecessary expense added up quickly.

"Cough or fever?"

"I sleep by the freeway, and all that goddamn dust gets to me."

Alice smiled. If Elaine wasn't cranky, she was probably sick.

"Sorry to hear that. Are you smoking?"

"I'm not going to quit."

Elaine was sixty-two years old, and for whatever reason, Alice just didn't think she looked entirely well. Alice thought she ought to check Elaine's blood counts, to be sure there wasn't evidence of infection or bleeding.

When the needles and tubes came out, Elaine yelled, "Jesus! I fuckin' told ya, I'm the same as always!"

Alice apologized after she drew blood, and then brought in a soda with ice to appease her. While Alice waited for the test results to come up, she called Copass on his cell phone to discuss the bed situation. Their conversation was brief. The hospital had dodged divert for the afternoon, and after hanging up she scribbled a quick note for Elaine's chart. To her relief, the blood counts were normal. For good measure she also checked Elaine's alcohol level, which was very much within her normal range. Alice wasn't sure why she had bothered checking, and then thought, *I'm just being paranoid since I can't admit anyone to the hospital.*

By the time she returned, Elaine had put on her shoes and was waiting in the hallway, arms crossed.

"Okay," Alice said. "Everything's normal, like you told me. See you next time."

"Thank you," Elaine said.

"Think about quitting smoking," Alice called after her. "Or cutting back."

"Give me a fuckin' break."

Frequent Flyers

When I came back to the wards at the beginning of the week, there were ten patients to start the morning with and fourteen total by the end of the day. Every time I discharged a patient, it seemed that two more came in to fill the space. Among the patients were a number who were on the mend, plus a guy with decompensated cirrhosis, a case of probable lung cancer, and a man strung out from a cocaine-opiate-methamphetamine party.

Around lunchtime Alice called to admit a homeless drinker named Fred Wirth, who was frequently in the ED for one thing or another and needed hospitalization for pneumonia this time. Wirth's chart was filled with records of his many ED and hospital visits. He had never made it to see a regular doctor in the clinics, so he saw somebody different every time he came in for medical care.

Among the medical problems in his chart was a festering foot ulcer, and the surgeons had recommended toe amputation to save the foot from further infection. Wirth had once visited the surgeons in the clinic and consented to a procedure to remove the toe, but then didn't show for the operation. After he "failed" that appointment, infection had spread to the bone. Then what happened? The chart didn't say, so I decided to ask Wirth myself.

"No, the toe is still there," he said. His face was red; he was not very drunk anymore and was beginning to look a little tremulous.

"In March, you came to the clinic and signed a permission slip for an operation."

He gave a blank stare. "I don't remember," he said. It was enough to make me wonder whether I'd read the wrong chart. How did you forget when a surgeon wanted to cut off your toe?

I put on gloves and removed Wirth's sneakers, which were swollen with mud and moisture, then peeled down his crusty socks. The toe was black, shriveled, and it looked like it would slough off on its own.

"Oh yeah," he said. "That thing." There weren't obvious signs of infection, though who could say what was happening beneath the surface? I poked the skin around the black toe and he watched dispassionately.

"Doesn't hurt or nothin'," he said.

I told him there could still be infected bone deep in the foot. He'd received a lengthy course of antibiotics, but it was still possible he would need surgery.

"No problem," he said.

I called his surgeons to let them know that Wirth was coming in-house, and that his gangrenous toe had dried up. Over the phone the surgeon said he was unlikely to operate, even if the bone was infected, at least not while the patient was hospitalized. We agreed this wouldn't get better on the streets, though, and he said he'd take a look. I thanked him and ordered a scan of the foot, which confirmed spread of the bone infection. A few days later, when Wirth was recovered from his pneumonia, the surgeons agreed to take him to the operating room right away, as soon as a space opened up. They'd send him to a nursing home afterward. *Hallelujah*, I thought. *He's getting fixed.*

In the afternoon, I admitted a patient named Jorge Gonzalez, a homeless man who had fevers, a nagging cough, and a little weight loss—he wasn't sure how much because he didn't own a scale, he said grumpily. Gonzalez's admission put my service again at fourteen, which for me was right around the point of maximum capacity. Fourteen made it a challenge to address every patient's every need, especially if one of the patients was sick and required constant attention. At fourteen—the number fluctuated through the day, as I discharged some and others came in—I began to think of the patients as "the guy with hepatic encephalopathy" or "the lady with pulmonary embolus." At one point I looked at the list and could not remember which last name went with which package of medical conditions. The non-urgent issues like high blood pressure and diabetes, and nutrition and vitamins, I left for the person's outpatient doctor, regardless of whether or not the patient had one.

With fourteen I was backed up. By the time I went to meet Gonzalez, he had already come to a private room on Three because he was assumed to be contagious until tests proved otherwise. My visit with him lasted less than five minutes; he told me right off the bat that he didn't want to be asked all the same questions all over again, didn't want me to examine his mouth and neck and stomach and ankles, because it had all been done a couple of times today already, and dozens of times in the past year. There wasn't much for me to do until the sputum microscopic results came back the following afternoon, so I didn't think about Gonzalez again until I was writing down his name and

hospital location and medication list for the evening resident, who could check on him overnight if needed.

Midweek, the hospital's census status remained stuck
on Code Purple level 2, which the hospital operators
announced over the hospital's public address system every
morning around eight o'clock. No one could really say
what Code Purple level 2 meant exactly, except that there
were no beds on Three and Four, and all of the potential
beds—beds currently occupied by patients who were likely
to be discharged—were already spoken for by ED patients
waiting to come up to the floors.

I began my morning rounds by seeing the patients I
was likely to discharge, so I could get the discharge process in motion. The first visit of the day was the patient
with hepatic encephalopathy, who had come out of his liver
stupor and was clear enough to tell me he was hungry. I
put on gloves and pulled out his nasogastric tube, through
which he'd been receiving a medication to clean ammonia
from his blood.

"We'll get you some breakfast and discharge you this
afternoon, as long as lunch goes okay," I said.

He said, "I'm pretty tired. I think I need an extra day."
He was homeless, I remembered.

"I know you're tired, but your blood tests are back to normal. I'll check on whether there's room at the respite center."
Sometimes doctors kept a homeless person hospitalized for
an extra day or two, because a recovering homeless person
could get sicker without a place to rest, and if discharged
might bounce right back to the hospital, which was neither
good for the hospital nor for the patient. In general I found
that patients really did feel better if you gave them an extra
day. However, on that day the county was jam-packed, and
we weren't in the *hospitality* business. I reassured myself that

at the respite center, he would be able to lie down and rest the entire day, rather than constantly move around on the streets to stay ahead of cops and predators.

"I'll go to respite," he said.

On the phone, Barb told me that respite wouldn't take him if he didn't need a nurse, which he didn't—he just needed to take his medication and lie down somewhere. She went to tell him that he could go to the infirmary at the DESC. He declined, said he'd rather go to the streets, said he had a spot where the cops wouldn't bother him.

A number of patients leaving Harborview refused to go to the shelters upon discharge. When I'd visited the DESC, the largest shelter downtown, my impression was that the facilities were a lot better than nothing. There was a large dayroom, showers, and two brand-new sleeping porches that were considerably warmer than the streets. Patients had made it clear to me, though, that the atmosphere changed when everybody piled in. There were too many drunks, too much in the way of drugs, fights, and mental illness, too much ruckus, too many rules, and above all your stuff could get stolen from under you while you slept. In order to continue staying at the shelter, you had to queue up every evening at 5 p.m. and hope you got a spot, which meant that a person really had no idea from day to day where he would be spending the night. Many preferred to camp under a highway overpass or sleep in a park or doorway, regardless of the weather.

So I wrote the patient's paperwork, and after lunch he went out the door. I was so busy that I didn't get by to say farewell, to remind him to visit his clinic doctor, but the truth was that I was also a little ashamed to be sending him out so fast. I didn't want to give him another chance to beg to stay another night, because I would probably cave, like I always did.

At noon I broke away from the wards to go to the faculty meeting, where Scott Barnhart was wearing a suit and a serious face. Scott had attended on the general medicine wards recently, despite the tremendous time that his administrative role demanded, and I had seen how deeply he felt the challenges of personally providing care for the poor and indigent. I had also recently learned that Scott's office was a low-key affair located off the main first-floor hallway, looking out onto Ninth Avenue, and that this space offered very little to buffer him from the public, which included the occasional homeless person overnighting in the old hospital lobby. In any case, he began the meeting by saying, "The good news is that our revenue is slightly ahead of budget for the year. We've exceeded projected volumes and income every month and in every category except outpatient visits. Trauma and burn numbers continue to grow."

Click. "The big change for the hospital is that the charity care load has expanded substantially," he said. The bar graph showed charity care dollars spent at the county: $35 million in 2001, $40 million in 2002, $54 million in 2003, $93 million in 2004, $98 million in 2005. The most charity care that any other hospital in metropolitan Seattle did in 2005 was $13 million, Scott said, and this was still substantially more than the rest of the pack. My pager rang.

"We can't sustain this kind of growth and continue to meet our bottom line," Scott continued. "As you know, we run on a razor-thin margin of less than 1 percent, and we do it with very little direct government support."

This was news to me.

"We've started having conversations with the other hospitals, apprising them of the situation and asking how they can help."

My pager rang again and I hurried out of the room while Scott entertained comments about the rising charity care numbers. The pages were from Barb, calling to tell me that she'd found a nursing home for one of the patients and could have him out the door in an hour and a half, if I could get the paperwork done right away.

"Can we push back by an hour?"

"He has a couple hours to travel, so they say that would be too late in the day. If you want later, we'd have to send him tomorrow."

"Fine, I'll do the paperwork now," I said. I stopped back into the meeting, where some of the faculty were talking about universal health coverage, and helped myself to a plate of salad, then returned to the wards. By afternoon I'd discharged six patients, a banner day that put my service back in single-digit range, but I still needed to see the two patients who'd been admitted and tucked in by the overnight resident. The first was a man who had bounced back from a bad bout of stomach flu and was waiting for me in his street clothes, ready to leave. I offered him a prescription medication for nausea, which he accepted gratefully, then I signed his discharge orders. I moved on to see Hope Sheridan, a fifty-year-old woman with breast cancer who had been admitted to the hospital for a blood clot, which had probably been caused by her cancer. She had a bed in the observation unit behind the ED, which was basically a long ward with ten beds and pink curtains that could be drawn around each for visual privacy. She was in the bay farthest from the nursing station. When I pulled back her curtain, she was propped up in bed with her eyes closed. Her boyfriend was sitting at her bedside, the chair positioned so that he blocked anyone from getting to the patient, and he was eating her lunch.

He looked up from the tray and said to me, "She ain't hungry." He had cleaned her plate and was chewing on the remains of the salad. I watched him scrape each of the carrot slivers from the bottom of the dish as I came around the opposite side of the bed, lifted the small television out of the way, and asked her how she was doing. She opened her eyes languidly, but didn't make eye contact with me.

Her boyfriend said, "She ain't getting enough pain medication. She's hurting." I asked her to point to where she was hurting.

"Her lungs are killing her," the boyfriend said.

I asked, "Is your pain where the tumor is?"

She squeaked out an answer: "Here." She lifted her trembling hand to her heart.

"How is your breathing?"

"Why don't you do something for her instead of asking all these questions?" the boyfriend said angrily. He had enormous hands.

"What would you suggest we do?"

He just shook his head and snorted.

I said, "I'd like you to leave while I examine Hope."

The boyfriend scraped the chair back two feet, which still blocked access to that whole side of the bed. "Good enough?"

I stared at him and raised my eyebrows, but he didn't get the hint. "You need to leave while I examine her," I said. With a jerk of my head, I indicated that he should move into the hallway.

The boyfriend pushed Hope's food tray away and stood. The fork clattered onto the floor. Hope closed her eyes. If I didn't know that nurses and security staff with their muscles and walkie-talkies would come running if I just raised my voice, I would feel at this man's mercy. He had to be two feet taller and almost three times my weight.

He snorted again, ripped his jacket off the back of the chair, and headed out the door.

I pulled the curtain around Hope's bed as soon as the door closed behind him and turned back to her. My heart was racing, but I didn't think I would be able to help very much if she saw that I was afraid of him, so I smiled cheerfully and made myself think about her breast cancer and blood clot.

There were three patients bunked close by, and it was likely that they'd heard the whole exchange with the boyfriend, so I lowered my voice and asked if she felt safe at home. The patient murmured something indeterminate. I asked whether she felt safe in the hospital, and she nodded yes.

While examining her, I noticed prominent bruises on her legs and hips.

"What's this?" I asked. She mumbled something about the blood thinner we were using to treat her blood clots, and added that she was just a clumsy person. But by appearance, the bruises looked days old, like something that had clearly happened before her hospitalization. It wasn't good that she denied domestic violence in the face of what seemed to be fairly obvious evidence.

The resident who had admitted her offered to have her listed under a pseudonym when she got a bed upstairs—a tactic used for celebrities, for the newsworthy, and anyone who might be in danger. We could speak about her condition only with her adult daughter, who earlier had brought in some soups and spoon-fed her mother, as though she were a child. But Hope didn't want to be concealed, and she indicated that we should update her boyfriend if he asked.

The resident wanted to put her under an assumed name anyway, and we sat in my office and debated the merits. My opinion was that if Hope said she felt safe in the hospital, we had to trust her. There were plenty of people around, which meant that he couldn't hurt her too badly here. What we needed to focus on was convincing her that there was a real problem, and getting her somewhere besides her abusive home when she left the hospital.

In any case, the resident arranged for Hope to be moved to a bed that was right in view of the nurses working at the observation desk. It made everybody feel better, except for the boyfriend, who got mad as hell. Hope would need the intravenous blood thinner for at least a few days, we told him. For everybody else, this meant there would be time to plot an escape strategy with her.

I saw Jorge Gonzalez in respiratory isolation last, because it took time to find a space hood that fit me, to don the filter and adjust the waist belt, and finally to open and shut the negative airflow chambers before entering his room. I had to give him the news that he was infectious and would need to remain isolated until he was no longer coughing up tuberculosis bugs anymore, which could be anywhere from a few days to several months, which to me sounded not unlike being placed in solitary confinement in jail.

I had no idea how Gonzalez would take the news. He was homeless, so he might be perfectly happy to have somewhere to stay, but he also might say we were holding him against his will. The other task I had to accomplish was to get him to agree to an HIV test, since some patients who came to the hospital with tuberculosis had underlying HIV, and often didn't get better unless the HIV was treated. I doubted that he was going to take this request well.

It was nearly five o'clock in the evening, but I put off seeing Gonzalez for a few minutes longer, in order to return some pages and write orders that the consulting services had recommended for other patients. A surgery resident called to tell me that Wirth, the drinker with the bone infection, had been discharged without an operation. He'd been bumped from the OR schedule, owing to a heavy night of incoming trauma. None of the elective cases got done, the resident told me, and he would have had to keep Wirth hospitalized for another five days, until his team had an opening on their elective procedure schedule.

"We told him in no uncertain terms that that this would worsen if he didn't follow up. He understands," the surgeon told me.

"Well, you're not the first person to tell him that," I said. The surgery resident was right, though, Wirth couldn't sit around for five days when there were dozens of people waiting for his bed. I had my own fresh crop of patients in the ED who needed space, including a homeless paraplegic named Amadou Gooding, who was frequently in and out of the hospital with a leg ulcer that never healed, because he lived on the streets and was always on his feet.

Gooding was a guaranteed rock, I knew, which was to say that he was a patient who would be around the wards for a while. His ulcer went so deep it hit near bone. Because Gooding was a former injection drug user, and because no nursing home in the city accepted patients with those credentials, he would probably have to be in the hospital for his six weeks of antibiotics.

In any case, Gonzalez had very little to say to me about the diagnosis I brought him and the plan for an HIV test and continued respiratory isolation. I asked him if there was anything he needed, and he asked for another blanket, because it got so cold in his room.

The hospital census remained high for the remainder of the week. Those who came into the hospital improved, went home, and were replenished on a daily basis by the newest patients coming in-house. Most days I saved Gonzalez for last on my rounds, since his condition seemed stable, and since he would swear at me whenever my visit lasted more than a few minutes. Perhaps because my attentions were relatively brief, he never seemed to remember who I was, even after I told him that his HIV test was negative. The only things he talked to me about were how much he hated my cold hands; how bad the food was; how neglected he was by his family, who never came to see him; and how he really hated George W. Bush, whom he blamed for his homelessness.

Among the patients who came and went that week were two patients who had overdosed with Tylenol, one of whom was a pretty young Vietnamese woman who had come to the United States by marriage. Her husband looked to be at least twenty-five years older than her, and when she was alone in the room, I asked about her safety. She turned red and said that they fought, but that her husband didn't hit her. She had very little to say to me about her relationship, or about the suicide attempt, over which she was thoroughly mortified. She agreed willingly, though, to mental health counseling to help adjust to living in America, and after three days of swallowing a foul-tasting syrup to protect her liver, she went home, and back to work that night in the restaurant that she and her husband ran together.

Hope Sheridan, the patient with breast cancer and bruises, was ready to go home by the end of the week. She had started to talk and smile, thanks mostly to her daughter, who brought her own young girls to visit every day with their grandmother. The daughter was determined to take her mother home, where she could be safe, where there would be someone else to call the police if "that horrible man came anywhere near." The day before she was to leave the hospital, Hope removed her bandana, cleaned herself up, and put on earrings, and when I walked by, I heard her giggling with her family. The safety plan for discharge was set.

But the following morning, the patient disappeared before the discharge paperwork and prescriptions were quite ready. Her daughter called in a panic, wanting to know what had happened to her. She called again a couple of hours later to report that she'd located her mother at her old home, with her abusive partner.

On the day that my census hit sixteen patients, I didn't see Gonzalez until six o'clock at night. He was dozing and grumpy when I tried to wake him to talk to me, so I listened to his lungs and then buzzed off, per his requests. There wasn't anything to do for him; he just needed to keep swallowing the pills and hope that the bacilli would start to clear. I tried to feel some sympathy for him, tried to imagine what it was like to be in a place where everyone who visited was wearing a space helmet. It had to be a lonely existence, particularly when no family or friends came to visit.

In the morning, Gonzalez was unresponsive when I rounded, and panted as though he couldn't get enough oxygen.

Twenty minutes later, Gonzalez was intubated and headed for the ICU. I received a call from his girlfriend—he had a girlfriend?—demanding to know what had happened, why no one had checked on him, why it took so long to pick up the aspiration pneumonia that had sent him to intensive care. I spent an hour talking with her in the waiting room, and she seemed to understand what we talked about, but the ICU resident called me later in the day to say that the girlfriend had a bunch of questions for me. They were the same questions she had asked that morning.

I mentioned the case to a colleague, who said, "How interesting. Last time he was here, he asked Barb to remove her as his legal decision-maker. He claimed she was stealing his money, and then she'd kicked him out of their apartment. He was homeless because of her." I hadn't known any of this—the story was probably in his chart—but I'd just been too preoccupied with getting people admitted, cared for, and discharged. I'd gotten too busy to be a very good advocate for the patients.

When Gonzalez's aunt decided to withdraw life support in the ICU a week later, the resident called to let me know what was happening. He had been sick enough to die, it was true, but I felt terrible all the same. I hadn't recognized how ill the patient was, and under my watch, he had become sicker. I had let myself be falsely reassured by how little he said, by how little he seemed to want what we were doing for him.

After Gonzalez died, his girlfriend called me to ask the same questions that she had asked the first morning I'd talked with her. These were the same questions she'd asked the ICU residents during his ICU course. It seemed I would never be able to satisfy her, no matter how many times I took on her queries, and then I never heard anything more from her. But I never forgot the patient himself, or how the grind finally got the better of me.

Closed for the Season

On a Monday morning in the middle of September the house hit 102 percent occupancy, thanks to a long weekend of attempted suicides, falls from rooftops and windows, construction accidents, and the usual stabbings and freeway-speed motorcycle crashes. The week's forecast called for sunshine and temperatures in the 80s—trauma weather—which meant the freeways and bike trails and sidewalks would flood with people trying to take in the last good weather of the summer.

On Monday night, the surgery side got killed. It was a particularly bad day for relationships, with two domestic stabbings and a strangulation assault that left three blotchy purple finger marks on the patient's neck plus little slivers of dried blood where fingernails gained purchase. Alice urged the patient to make a report, told her that choking was often the sentinel event before a fatality, but the patient declined having her injuries photographed by police. She had a plan for escape, she told Alice, and she took a cab to her sister's house.

Between trauma resuscitations, the on-call surgery residents personally pushed the emergency cases downstairs to the ORs, and after the cases finished at 4 a.m., the residents opted to ride the elevators two floors up to the ED in order to gain a thirty-second respite from the chaos.

The Tuesday morning census miraculously stayed even, and there were just three patients in the ED awaiting a positive bed. By then, though, the sun had been up for hours, and at lunchtime the ED filled with bodies mangled by backhoes and trucks and felled trees, bodies shipped to the hospital via air ambulance from east of the Cascade Mountains, from ranches in Montana, and from coastal Alaskan hospitals. In the evening, there was a pedestrian-versus-car accident, two patients with gunshot wounds to the torso— same incident—and a flood of smaller dings, including an infected-looking hand wound inflicted by a kitchen knife. The patient, a line cook, really should have been admitted to the hospital, but he declined on a financial basis: he had no insurance and would have to pay out of pocket, and he would lose his job if he missed work.

When Alice came in at 6 a.m. on Wednesday, the morning census showed the hospital at eight negative beds, significantly less capacity for a Wednesday morning than could be good for the hospital, especially with the temperature predicted to peak on Friday. At four in the afternoon, the lineup of stretchers at the triage desk backed all the way out to the ambulance ramp, and everything jammed up when a sixteen-year-old who had nearly drowned came in the door, a paramedic performing chest compressions astride the boy as the stretcher was wheeled into the trauma suite. Even though everything happened as quickly and smoothly as possible and they got the kid back, it was still forty minutes before the ICU was ready to take him, which meant forty minutes before things were humming again in the ED and Alice was headed to meet with Scott.

Downstairs, the Board showed utter gridlock, and the air traffic nurse lamented that most of the day's discharges were already accounted for, that the twelve people waiting for beds in the ED and environs would be moving upstairs by late afternoon.

"Two and a half days to the weekend," Scott said, by which he meant two and a half days until there was even less capacity to speak of. "I don't like it. We'll start screening transfers from other hospitals and focus on the mission populations, and look at divert tomorrow if things don't start to loosen up."

Scott had threatened divert previously and it hadn't happened, which Alice thought was a good thing. She believed Copass's line that Harborview's reputation in the community was paramount, and that the reputation could take a hit if the hospital became one that did not always take everyone who came to the door. Shortly afterward, Alice called a huddle in the ED to let the residents and attendings know about the bed situation. She told them to think hard about admissions, to try to get the homeless to shelters, and send the subacute patients for a recheck the following day in the clinics. If the clinics couldn't see them, she said, they could come back to the ED. Copass called Alice on her cell phone as she was driving home and said he didn't think the hospital would close, said he didn't think they could just turn people away.

"Divert will put us behind," he said. "It'll be weeks of trying to catch up with everyone who's gotten sicker in the meantime."

Alice said, "Hopefully we're over the hump."

On Thursday morning, the ED was quiet and the census email talked optimistically of six positive beds.

Alice walked through the observation unit and noted a handful of boarders, many of whom looked ready for discharge. Copass was in a good mood during rounds. He told jokes about the doctors and stories about the patients as he read through the charts. The residents, who were all female that day, laughed politely. Alice's cell phone remained notably silent.

At ten o'clock there was a multiple-vehicle pileup on I-5, near the Georgetown neighborhood in southwest Seattle, which brought two unstable trauma patients via medic unit, including one with life-threatening bleeding in the pelvis, plus three more patients who looked pretty bruised but had no major fractures. Fifteen minutes later, the medics fetched a woman in West Seattle who had collapsed at home, and then a man in the Central District who was having terrible, crushing chest pain.

The ED whiteboard filled with red marker for surgery patients, and then with blue marker for medicine patients. Everyone was sick, it seemed. Some needed the OR immediately and a number required observation, if not outright hospitalization. By noon the positive beds were full and the discharges were proceeding at a sluggish pace. The cell phone rang.

Alice took the call and said, "I'll be there in a few minutes." She was teaching a medical student how to draw arterial blood from the wrist; the patient was having an asthma exacerbation, and she wanted to see the patient breathing more comfortably before she left the department.

By the time Alice got to the Board, the bed situation was eleven negative, and Scott was resolute. He said, "I think the right thing is to go on divert this afternoon and see if we can catch up by morning. This gives us tomorrow to discharge, so we can try to stay open through the weekend. Alice, we'll have to communicate with the private ambulance companies that we're only doing trauma at this point. Everyone else will have to be transported to another hospital."

Alice sighed. She knew that the private ambulances wouldn't be happy with this decision. She knew the ED attendings would ask which hospitals would be taking Harborview's transfers, and she knew that as soon as they went on divert, the phone harassment would begin, the questions from other facilities about when the hospital would be opening back up. Above all she knew that Copass's good mood would sour, not only for the afternoon, but for days to come. She knew he would take it as a personal failure that Harborview was turning patients away.

Her first stop was the radio room, where one of the computer screens showed that every other hospital in the city had open beds. She took a deep breath and decided those facilities could take care of patients just as well. On the computer screen Harborview's box had already turned red, signifying that the hospital was closed to transfers, and seeing this made Alice's heart sink. She marched out of the radio room and called a huddle in the Fishbowl. Some of the attendings had questions about which patients would get to stay and which would become potential transfers, and Alice opined that anyone who'd received their primary care from the Harborview system had priority.

At first, the sick patients went to the shelters. When the shelters filled, the patients went to the streets, and then they came back to the ED some hours later, if the streets didn't work out. But by the time Alice was back in the radio room in the early evening, the hospital inflow had subsided, and air traffic was making headway with the bed situation: there were a couple of positive beds available for patients requiring urgent surgery.

Alice glanced at the computer screen that showed the area hospital bed census and saw that two more hospitals had turned red, and that there was more yellow than earlier in the day. She wondered what was happening in the city and made a mental note to watch the evening news. As she left the hospital, she was optimistic that Harborview would come off divert in the morning. She was even coming to terms with Scott's preemptive attempt to turn back the floodwaters before things got completely out of hand.

E ven though the hospital was on divert, plenty of patients still came to the ED, including an eighty-year-old named Montel Menino, a cheerful man who went to visit his doctor in Reno, Nevada, and never returned home. The cops told Alice he had taken the bus to Boise and from there to Seattle. For all Alice knew, he could have ended up right back in Reno if the Seattle police hadn't apprehended him at the bus terminal. Naturally, he had been brought to Harborview for evaluation, which meant that his ride home was now the hospital's problem.

Alice said that Menino knew his name, but had no idea where he was. His physical exam and labs were normal. He was suffering from fairly advanced dementia, and there was nothing acutely wrong with him, she said, except that the ED couldn't just let him walk out the door. He'd subsisted on chips for the last four days and wolfed down his pancakes and eggs in the ED, and fifteen minutes later he had asked for breakfast again, forgetting that he'd just eaten.

In addition to Menino, Alice wanted me to admit an elderly woman named Karen Chow, whose lungs had been burned badly in a big fire that morning. She arrived smelling like a barbecue pit, Alice said, and had screamed with pain until they had pushed some heavy-duty pain meds.

"The patient has end-stage cancer and has been very clear that she never wanted aggressive measures in any situation," Alice said. The plan was to send her to Three for comfort care, which would involve a continuous drip of intravenous pain medication until she passed away.

"The medics brought her here because she was a burn patient," Alice said. "She usually gets her care at a private hospital, and given the circumstances, we thought about trying to transfer her there, but she's breathing pretty hard and I don't think it will be long."

I thanked her and went to find Menino, who had the potential to be in-house for a while. He was boarding in the back of the ED's east wing, in a little L-shaped room with four beds partitioned off by curtains. A hospital gown peeked out from underneath his flannel shirt and khaki pants.

"I want to go home," he said, and broke into a little bit of Spanish—I think he was saying that someone was taking his checks—and then in English he told me that he was hungry. He continued to chatter away merrily even as I listened to his heart and lungs.

"Any pain? Any stomach problems?"

"*Pero no*," he said. "Can I go home?"

"Any chest pain?"

"No. I want to go home."

"Do you want to go back to the nursing home where you were living?"

"Yes, please."

"How will you get there?"

"I will take a bus."

I called Barb immediately. He didn't know the name of the facility where he was living in Reno, and seemed to have no idea whether he even had any living family. The only thing that seemed certain was that he had no one who could accompany him back to his nursing home in Nevada.

Barb said that his travel arrangements would probably include ambulances, airport escorts, and a two-hour direct flight, to make sure he didn't wander off and end up in Chicago next. There was also the question of whether we could put a demented patient on an airplane without obtaining somebody's permission, and there was the question of who exactly that person would be.

"He says he wants to go back to the nursing home, and that they treat him well there," I said. "That's probably all we need to know."

I stopped by a bed in the observation unit to see a young man with a resolving leg infection who looked ready to leave, and I sat for a moment and cranked out his paperwork and prescriptions. As I was finishing his hospital summary, Menino's nurse paged to say, "Did you tell him he could go home?"

"Barb is working on his arrangements. It might take a couple of days."

"Because he thought his doctor said he could go, so he got up and left. The security people brought him back from the espresso cart."

I was laughing.

She said, "Yeah. So I told him he isn't going anywhere and he just needs to wait at his bed. I'll call you again if I need to tie him down."

Upstairs I found Karen Chow, the elderly lady who had been burned in the fire, in a private room. She was getting intravenous morphine at 30 milligrams per hour, and she was still breathing hard, at thirty-four times per minute. Her family surrounded the bed. A son who was stroking her wrist raised his eyebrows when I came in. Later he told me that his mother's face had been burned so badly, the family had identified her by an old broken toe.

"I sort of thought she might have passed on by now," he said.

I nodded. "I'm surprised that she's still breathing so hard. She's getting a healthy dose of morphine."

The son looked liked he hadn't slept. He said, "Can't you do something? To hasten things? Mom's breast cancer is in her bones and her liver, and she's lived with really bad pain. I mean, she's been ready to go for a while. She *never* wanted to be alive like this."

"We can't really do anything to *hasten* her death, legally, but we can continue to increase the morphine drip so she isn't breathing so rapidly."

"Will that do anything?"

"Well, the goal of therapy is to make her more comfortable while her body naturally begins to shut down. We're not trying to *hasten* anything. But it happens that increasing the morphine drip is what you'd do in either case."

The patient's sister smiled.

"I understand," she said.

I listened to her lungs and heart and took her pulse. All was normal, which confirmed that she was still some way from dying, even though it had been twenty-four hours since the fire. I offered to transfer her to the private hospital where she'd been previously, but the family was quick to reassure me that they were happy with the care, they just didn't want Mom to keep suffering. I went out to the nurses' station and requested a large morphine bolus, to be repeated in six hours if she continued to be that uncomfortable.

Her nurse said, "That's a big dose."

I told her I would stand at the bedside and push the drugs myself, if she wanted.

The nurse asked, "Are you sure?"

"The family really feels like she's suffering, and she is breathing very hard." I had told the family that the patient was sedated and shouldn't be feeling anything.

The nurse said she'd do the first one if I would come by in a little while to check on things, so I agreed, and moved on. My total for the morning was four discharges—three positive beds on the wards upstairs and a negative bed in the ED. By the time Alice convened with Scott at the air traffic control desk, the situation was considerably more fluid: the hospital now had several positive beds, and the discharges were expected to keep coming through the afternoon and into the evening. Alice and the air traffic nurse looked pleased, but Scott shook his head and said the hospital would stay on divert; they would reevaluate later in the day.

"Twelve beds is not enough to reopen on," he said, because those beds would be filled in the first hours of the weekend by trauma and burn cases. He didn't think the hospital would last off divert more than a few hours.

Alice was of the opinion that the hospital should reopen when it could, but the decision was Scott's, so she followed orders and went back to the ED to reaffirm that private ambulances were to continue transporting patients elsewhere. In the radio room, the hospital census screen now showed all of the area hospitals closed to transfers—an entire screen of red—and Alice didn't understand how the hospitals had gone from plenty of capacity to nothing overnight, since most ran at about 65 percent occupancy. Copass materialized in the radio room and avoided making eye contact with her. He moved about mutely, shuffled some piles of paper, and then finally pointed to the computer screen and whispered, "That is complete bullshit."

He snatched a walkie-talkie off the counter, put it on his waist, and walked out of the room.

Yeah, Alice thought, *it showed that when the safety net got into trouble, everything could come grinding to a halt.* There was now no capacity anywhere in the city, and ambulances were driving considerable distances to get patients to care.

Soon, the administration learned that the other hospitals had closed in response to Harborview's closing, despite the available beds, and Scott and his deputies spent the day placing phone calls to various administrative offices in hospitals around the city, explaining that Harborview had fewer than zero beds, that patients were waiting on stretchers for admission, that the hospital simply didn't have the capacity to run all of the services and tests for every patient who came to the ED. He suggested, as gently as he could, that Harborview would have a hard time opening up again until others took up some of the slack.

Up on the wards, Karen Chow looked no different by the end of the afternoon. Her sister still sat by the bed; other family members had gone in search of coffee and food. The sister said she wasn't hungry.

"You better go home and get some sleep."

"I want to be here when she dies." Then she started crying and squeezed Karen's hand. "Every breath she takes smells like smoke, like she was burned on the inside. It's so horrible."

I waited uncomfortably until she stopped crying, and then I said, "The nurse can call you when her breathing starts to slow down. There will be some advance warning before she dies."

This cheered her, and she said again how wonderful she thought everyone had been. I told her I would order another increase in the morphine drip, which was within the usual comfort care protocol, and I reassured her that her sister would pass by the morning—I was sure of it.

Downstairs, Alice was wrapping up her day, and just before she left, she saw that the hospital census Web site in the radio room had transformed from solid red to blocks of yellow and green.

How very interesting, she thought.

By the weekend, I had coaxed a few more people out the door: a homeless man whose skin abscess had improved, a young woman who had passed a kidney stone, a guy with HIV whose unexplained fever seemed to have resolved. The only one I hadn't managed to get out the door was Amadou Gooding, the man with the leg ulcer. He was in the fourth of his six weeks of intravenous antibiotics, and was still in-house because no nursing home wanted him. He had a history of suicide attempts and hospitalizations on file, and his prior injection drug use deterred every nursing facility in the greater Seattle area. He was a complicated enough case that he had been adopted by the extreme team for social work, which took on the patients who were notoriously difficult to place in nursing homes.

I liked Gooding, even though others found him difficult sometimes. For one thing, he always said thank you. Some days he brought me fruit from the cafeteria, and it amused me that as he handed me an orange or a banana he always said, "You probably don't eat junk food." What I liked most was that he seemed to understand his medical problems and wanted to do whatever it took to get them fixed.

I didn't know Gooding's real story, and I didn't think I wanted to know. It was very possible that his answers would affect how I took care of him. Earlier in his stay, he told me that rivals were trying to displace him from his corner. He was a panhandler, he said, and he made money by singing outside Symphony Hall. I'd heard that panhandlers made decent money, all things considered, but more than once I saw him change from his patient gown into new, fashionable clothing, and I wasn't sure that Gooding could make the kind of money he was spending from panhandling alone.

I knew that drug dealers came to Harborview for medical care. I knew I took care of them, although I didn't always know who they were. Sometimes this information was in the charts of the ornery, stereotypical patients, but I was sure there were others I didn't know about. Gooding struck me as the sort of individual who had the charisma and intelligence and hustle of someone who could have run a legitimate company, if only he had been pointed in the right direction much earlier in his life. Anyway, my hunch was that he would have been happy to stay at Harborview for months if we would let him, that he wanted things to cool down on the streets before he returned. So I listened without challenging him, and he always thanked me for stopping by to talk.

On Saturday morning, Alice noted that the hospital had continued to fill despite being on divert. She was working the phones in the ED, coordinating patients with the hospital's transfer center, which handled incoming requests from outside doctors looking to send patients to Harborview. Early in the afternoon, a call came through from a nephrologist in the south Puget Sound, which was outside of King County, about a patient he wanted to transfer for dialysis.

"I'm sorry, but we're not accepting transfer patients at the moment," Alice said.

There was a pause, and the doctor said, "What?"

"We've run out of beds, so we're not able to take transfers right now."

"That's completely inappropriate! I've been there before, and I know how it works! Boy, I pay a lot of tax to keep you people open," the doctor screamed.

"Look, don't you have a way to perform dialysis in an emergency situation?" Alice asked.

"We don't have the staffing this weekend!" the doctor screamed.

Alice wondered whether the patient was uninsured. There were at least a half-dozen hospitals in the vicinity of the doctor, all of which were closer to him.

"Listen, I'm really sorry, but the reason we can't take him is that we don't have the *space*. And urgent dialysis is something that other hospitals can help with."

"I can't believe this crap," the doctor scoffed. "I've never had a problem with you people before, but this is ridiculous. Who is the supervisor there?"

Alice said, "I'm the supervisor today. The people who usually take the physician calls are seeing patients. So I guess I would suggest that you try one of the hospitals near you. Each of them has capacity."

"Ridiculous," the doctor snorted and hung up. Alice carefully replaced the phone in its cradle, her hands shaking. She didn't understand why some physicians couldn't see the big picture, couldn't see that there were so many uninsured patients that no single hospital could handle all of them.

She wanted to call back this doctor and lecture him, but the call was over. Alice had violated Copass's second commandment—Be polite—but she didn't care then, even if she might care later on. The whole afternoon, she thought of things she should have said, comebacks she might have used. Eventually she calmed down and told herself it was good she hadn't said more. Still, she didn't think doctors should be allowed to drive their comfortable cars and pull down $250,000-plus every year, and be given free license to avert their eyes from a broken health care system.

Alice fielded a few more phone calls, declining other hospitals' requests to transfer their patients—including an obese patient with resistant lung disease, and another with a sickle cell anemia crisis confined to the patient's shoulder ("Since you guys are the experts," the caller said, which was code for "since you take the difficult, poor patients who get sickle crisis"). She directed both callers to the private hospitals, because anyone could give pain meds and fluids for sickle cell crisis. Maybe because she'd had her big battle for the day, she found a way to be firm without going into the details of the bed situation. And perhaps because the doctors heard the sharp edge in her sweet voice, they did as she asked.

The following morning, Alice told me that Fred Wirth, the drinker with the gangrenous foot, was back.

"I'm bringing him in," Alice said.

"How did he get here?"

"He walked. We can't really stop patients from walking in."

"He's walking on that thing?"

"Yeah," she said.

I knew Wirth from before, so I told Alice I would take him again. It was doubtful he'd get the definitive surgery he needed, given the pressure on beds. But he had a touch of congestive heart failure, a condition I could actually fix, at least temporarily. Wirth again had no memory of me; when I went to see him, he was just starting to come down off his buzz. I put on gloves and removed the shoes and tube socks that were sticking to his body. His black toe had begun melting away, but now he had a new, larger ulcer on his shin. I decided we'd talk about surgery later, when he was sobered up and might remember something.

Upstairs, Karen Chow was again breathing at twenty-four breaths per minute. Just a few family members were at her bedside today.

I said hello to everyone and then said, "Apparently, I can't knock her off." The family laughed.

"We all got some sleep," the son said. "Finally. Thank you."

Another relative said, "Maybe she's gotten used to the morphine. Maybe it doesn't affect her anymore?"

"That typically takes more than just a few days."

"Well, she had a patch before."

I put a hand to my forehead. I hadn't gotten this part of the story before. "The fentanyl patch. She's used to the really strong stuff."

"She would have been a good drug addict!" one of the men joked, and everybody laughed again.

I told the family that I hadn't seen a situation like this before, but it was possible that the IV fluid she was getting along with the morphine drip was flushing out her kidneys. I doubled her dose of morphine and said I'd double it again six hours later if she remained uncomfortable. I told them to call in the troops, because it was going to happen by the end of the day.

On Monday morning, Alice was standing on her toes in front of the Board with the air traffic control nurse, waiting for Scott. There could be forty-five open beds and perhaps more, owing to Karen Chow's peaceful passing overnight; to the ambulance that was taking Montel Menino to the airport, where he would catch a direct flight home to Reno; and to Fred Wirth's unannounced departure—his nurse discovered his abandoned hospital gown in his bed and the IV that he'd torn out of his arm, the tape with little hairs attached. Presumably, Wirth had headed back to the streets to drink because his chest felt marginally better, because he was starting to feel a little tremulous from his low blood alcohol level. A half hour later, air traffic control relinquished his bed.

Forty-five-plus discharges for the day meant the ED could begin to move hospital admissions to their various destinations, could go back to addressing medical emergencies. It meant that private ambulances could return to stabilizing and transporting, rather than selling patients to hospitals that weren't interested. It meant the county hospital's front door was open again for whoever wished to come in.

My service had been whittled down to a few overnighters plus Amadou Gooding, the singing panhandler, and it had been a nice hiatus from the busyness; in a few days, the service would be full again, and in the meantime, I'd gotten to spend time with the patients and their families.

"Divert seemed so easy to do, at least in hindsight," Alice told me when we were out for breakfast later that week. "We got caught up with the backlog. We had time to take care of people and weren't running around like crazy. But what about everyone who didn't get to the hospital in time?"

"Divert didn't exactly stop the admissions."

"No, but there were fewer. We'll always have admissions, because the only ones who get diverted are the private ambulances. The same patients we always get were walking into the ED, instead of coming by ambulance."

I told Alice I'd had a fairly relaxed weekend on divert.

"It's a different ball game when you turn people away," she said.

Catch and Release

Not long after Harborview came off divert, the hospitals in metropolitan Seattle met to hammer out a plan to ensure that there would always be emergency capacity across the city, so that ambulances could readily find a hospital nearby for their patients. The plan was called Treat and Transfer, and it went into effect when any hospital reached its limit on staffed beds. Under Treat and Transfer, a patient in the ED received the same medical attention as he otherwise would, and if he needed hospitalization, the ED attending would then identify another hospital in the city to admit him. This solution seemed fair enough, since there were seven large hospitals within a seven-mile radius, and this meant that an ED did not have to close to ambulances just because a hospital had no beds upstairs.

For Harborview, Treat and Transfer was a sleight of hand trick that allowed the hospital to close at 105 percent capacity but not turn anybody away at the front door, at least in theory. The reality was that when the census approached capacity, Harborview's beds were saved for potential trauma and burn patients, since Harborview was the only hospital in Washington State with 24/7 expertise in these specialties. The patients selected for transfer, therefore, were generally medicine patients, and this posed certain challenges for the ED attendings, who had renamed the plan Catch and Release. For years, Harborview's transfers had always been incoming and never outgoing, and physicians at other hospitals were not in the habit of saying yes to Harborview's medicine patients.

When a patient was selected for transfer, an attending such as Alice went into the radio room, checked the screen showing which hospitals were accepting patients, and began to make a series of calls, not unlike a bond salesman trying to unload an unfavorable position. She told the admitting doctor at the first hospital she targeted that Harborview needed to find a bed for a forty-five-year-old drinker with a fever, because they had no open beds. The first hospital said they'd get back to her, an ominous sign, and fifteen minutes later the answer came back, "We don't feel this patient is appropriate for us." Alice politely thanked the doctor for checking, then told him she would check around but would likely be calling back because they were genuinely out of beds. She hung up and sighed because she knew the doctor's refusal to take the patient wasn't for the complexity of the case—after all, if you couldn't take care of a drinker with a fever, what on earth could you take care of? The hospital had refused, most likely, because the patient had no health insurance.

The doctor at the second hospital balked by asking a lot of questions. This was a game Alice was familiar with, so she answered the questions truthfully, with a minimum amount of information, to try to keep the doctor from saying no. The longer she could keep him on the phone, the better the chance that he'd feel guilty and accept the patient.

Finally Alice told him, "You sound concerned that we're trying to dump this patient. The situation here is that we have ten people boarding in the ED, and we don't have anywhere to put him. That's why I'm calling." The doctor told her he'd call back with an answer. Frustrated, she hung up and hit the speed dial button for the university hospital, which was linked with Harborview by the medical school as well as a shared business office.

Recently the university hospital had decided to limit the number of beds for medicine patients to thirty-two. It did not matter if there were open beds elsewhere in the hospital. Surgical procedures simply paid better money, and there were very few patients requiring surgical procedures on the medicine service.

Alice had found that on average it took her nearly two hours to find another hospital that would accept a patient when Harborview was on Catch and Release. That was two hours that a patient sat in the crowded and uncomfortable emergency room, two hours that necessary hospital care might be delayed, and a lot of extra time that Alice spent hooked to the telephone when she could be taking care of patients instead.

The triage doctor for the university hospital came on line and began to ask all of the same questions, and then said, "Look, you get government money to take care of your patients, and we don't."

At this Alice straightened up, smiled and said, "Our hospital is full and we have ten patients boarding in the ED. It would be nice to see other people step up."

Naturally, Alice got into a little bit of trouble for talking this way to a doctor at another hospital, even though no one actually disagreed with the content of her speech. The administration advised her to try to work things out collegially and professionally with the other hospitals. Speak firmly and courteously and stick with facts, they told her.

"I think I was pretty factual," she said. The other members of the junta, who were male, told her that she was getting pushback because she was female; they made the same speeches.

At that, the hospital administration made a round of PowerPoint presentations about hospital volumes and charity care numbers. The word came back to the junta, to be shared with all of the ED attendings: the other hospitals would gladly take patients when we were on Treat and Transfer. We just needed to call.

One afternoon while Alice was managing the latest Catch and Release operation in the ED, Kermit Jackson returned with a fever, again threatening to kill everyone. She saw the discharge note I'd left in the computer and paged me to the Fishbowl.

"Your old friend, Agent K, is back," she said. She gave me a quick update on Catch and Release. The business people at the private hospitals might have a priori accepted the concept of transfers from Harborview, she said, but word didn't seem to have trickled down to the people actually seeing the patients. They continued to decline her transfer requests, for a variety of reasons.

Alice said she didn't want to spend time calling around, especially since Kermit was a friend of Fleet's. "He needs to come in," she said.

I'd be happy to take him, I said, especially since I knew him from last time.

"He'll get better care here," she said. "The private hospitals will send him back as soon as they can, anyway." She'd already talked to the air traffic control nurses at the Board and told them she was bringing Kermit in-house, despite the negative number of beds. There was some resistance from air traffic, and Alice responded that sending a homicidal patient would certainly burn any bridges they'd built with the other hospitals.

I found Kermit in the room right by the Fishbowl, where staff could keep an eye on him. I walked in and closed the curtain separating Kermit from his neighbor, a prisoner in a bright red jumpsuit whose right wrist and foot were locked to the gurney with a leather and metal restraint. A pudgy jail guard sat in a plastic chair at the prisoner's bedside, reading the newspaper.

"Hi, Kermit, it's me." I pulled the sheet off his face.

"Shit!" Kermit said. His eyes snapped open. Then he recognized me and said, "*Hey*, girl! How are you *doing*?"

"You're back, Kermit."

"Shit."

"You heard that you have a fever?"

"Shit."

"We'll bring you in-house for a couple of days."

"Shit."

I held Kermit's shoulder as I listened carefully to the crackles at the base of his right lung. Alice had said she thought he had pneumonia, and the diagnosis seemed clear enough from the exam and blood results. Kermit told me he didn't remember much of his last visit, and because the patient in the next bed had come from the jail, I was glad he didn't air his gripe about being held against his will. He was definitely more lucid than before and told me he'd been playing his horn. Moving to the sink to wash my hands, I said that we'd be hanging IV antibiotics. I realized that I was no longer afraid of him, perhaps because he seemed to trust me.

"You'll be here tomorrow?"

"I will see you tomorrow."

"Good," he said. He pulled the sheet up over his eyes, mumbled a few words, and then fell quiet. I noticed the horn case beside his bed, which had been packed up and labeled, and which was headed for his own personal locker upstairs.

I got the orders written and found Alice leaning on the far counter in the radio room, waiting for an incoming call from the medics. When the phone rang, she identified herself as the Medic One doctor and listened to the bullet. The medic asked permission to bring the patient to Harborview, and she asked whether the patient had ever been to one of the other hospitals. The medics told her he hadn't, and that they wanted to bring him in. She gave permission, then hung up and said into her walkie-talkie, "Medic One Doc to Charge and Triage, there is a forty-one-year-old male found down, responded to 0.4 of Narcan, with shallow respirations. ETA five minutes."

The walkie-talkie responded: "We don't have any beds, can the patient go somewhere else?"

"He's coming here," she told the walkie-talkie.

Alice had heard repeatedly from her husband, the paramedic, about the chilly reception that medics received from the private hospitals. Sometimes the hospitals made the medics, and therefore the patients, wait ten or fifteen minutes before a nurse or doctor came for a report on what had happened, which made the medics delay their next response to an incoming 9-1-1 call. Sometimes they'd even get yelled at by the ED staff at these hospitals.

Alice's husband felt that he did his job competently. He believed that his role was to stabilize sick patients for transport to the hospital, and to do so with as much courtesy and reassurance as he could offer. Because neither he nor any of the other paramedics felt comfortable waiting around the ten or fifteen minutes it sometimes took in the private EDs, he and his colleagues simply requested permission to bring all of their patients to Harborview, rich or poor, and almost always regardless of the diagnosis, because they knew that the patients would be cared for immediately and politely and well, every time.

That was the system as Copass had created it: his friendly and competent paramedics on the pre-hospital end, his polite and hardworking doctors and nurses on the ED end. That system was how all of the complicated traumas and burns, the big-money cases, had come to Harborview in the first place. That system boiled down to three simple precepts, three commandments enforced by an elderly neurologist with a twitchy cheek.

"Maybe Mr. Narcan won't need to be admitted," Alice said hopefully, and then she grinned. "Of course, the hospital has got plenty of space on Six. We would just need to make the private rooms into semiprivate. But whatever."

For most of my first year at Harborview, Six was the ward that lived behind a door I passed several times a day, on my way up and down the stairs between the medicine cases on Three and Four and the surgical or wound care cases on Seven and Eight. Six had private rooms for patients with the ability to scratch out personal checks for tens of thousands of dollars without checking their bank balance first. (This arrangement was *not* unique to Harborview.) It was not a ward where any of my own patients went very often, even when the hospital was full to the gills and air traffic was putting people wherever there was space.

That was a shame, because it was a lovely, quiet floor where you could always find the patient charts—and the patients, for that matter. There were often fresh flowers at

the front desk that a previous patient left behind for everyone to enjoy. The hallways were painted a soothing buttery
yellow, and the nurses were cheerfully solicitous and highly
competent in the care of postoperative orthopedic patients.

I got my first chance to work on Six when Scott Barnhart paged me to say that an orthopedic surgeon wanted an
evaluation for diabetes on a patient scheduled for lumbar
stabilization and fusion. Scott asked whether I thought I
could do this, and what could I say to Scott except yes?
The patient's name was Roger O'Brien, and he and his
wife, Rita, were waiting for me in the surgery clinic. They
were a retired couple who had traveled from their home
on the Olympic Peninsula, at the edge of the rain forest.
I explained that I was supposed to vet his heart and predict the risk of a medical complication after surgery. Roger
looked concerned.

"I'm nervous about this," he told me. He'd already had
two back surgeries; one didn't work and the other made
things better for three months, but currently he could only
walk to the mailbox before his leg pain was out of control.

"Your surgeon, Dr. Chapman, is the guy you want."

"Everyone says he's the best."

"He helps a lot of people."

"I just don't understand how he ended up in a place like
this," Roger said. "I mean, there's a guy sleeping in the
lobby. It's pretty interesting out there."

I explained how Harborview worked and told him that
complicated trauma cases and great surgeons went hand in
hand.

He nodded and seemed to agree with the idea of an egali-
tarian hospital, although it was also clear he did not want
to share a hospital room with the guy sleeping in the lobby.

I asked about Roger's health history and wrote down the number of his primary care doctor as well as the names and doses of medications that he had handwritten on a three-by-five inch index card in his wallet. I did an extensive physical examination, looking into his ear canals and shining a flashlight on his tonsils, studying his fingernails and palpating the neck, where the thyroid lives, even though it would be the heart and lung exams that would really have consequences for the proposed surgery. He had bad earwax in both of his ears, I told him, writing a prescription for some drops. I also told him that surgery would pose some risk to his heart, since he hadn't been physically active recently.

"That's what I'm worried about."

"There's always a risk with surgery. I think in your case the risk is average, and I'm going to tell the surgeon it's safe to go ahead." I was scribbling another prescription, this one for medication that could protect his heart during surgery. He liked this idea.

"I'll see you after the operation to make sure things go as well as possible," I told him.

"You'll see me?" he asked. His wife looked pleased. "Quite a system you have here."

The surgeons took Roger as the first case of the morning, and his epic procedure lasted until four o'clock in the afternoon. He sailed through surgery without a hitch, and I found him upstairs on Six the next morning. His room was like every other room in the hospital, with bays for two beds, but he got the whole thing to himself, and the space felt palatial. He was in a fair amount of pain when I visited, but he seemed relieved all the same that he had come through, and we chatted for a while before I signed off and wished him luck with rehabilitation.

As it turned out, it wasn't my last visit to Six. The calls from the surgeons started to arrive at a more or less steady pace, bringing enough business that the hospital hired two new doctors for the coming year to handle the surgical consultations alone. This foreshadowed what was to come: surgical procedures represented the financial future of every hospital in America.

Later in the day I was back on Four, and one of the hospital doctors flagged me down to report that Paul Brown had been in-house last week, that he'd gotten a job waiting tables at one of the family-style chain restaurants in his hometown, and was even dating someone. Paul was in and out in two days, she told me, for something that turned out to be nothing. He never asked for pain medication, she said.

I smiled at the news and realized it had been a while since I'd seen him in the hospital, and then I moved onward to see Kermit, whose first question was when I was going to go out with him.

"You better come hear me play at the club," he said.

"Sure, I'll think about it."

"Monday night, eight o'clock. Bring your husband, have a drink, and enjoy the show."

The dialysis nurses told me they'd listened to Kermit's records, that he really was talented, that he'd played with Miles Davis and other legendary musicians. It wasn't clear to me how Kermit would get to the club, given that he lived in a nursing home fifteen miles south of the city and had no ready mode of transportation, but I didn't raise these finer points with him.

When I returned to discuss the medications he would be getting at discharge, he had changed into a suit, tie, and matching bowler hat. He was seated in a chair by the bed and lurched drunkenly to his left side.

"Kermit?" I put my hand out to steady him; he looked as though he might continue leaning leftward until he hit the ground.

His eyes fluttered open for a moment, then rolled back into his head.

"Mr. Jackson, are you okay?" He appeared to be breathing. I checked his pulse at his wrist; it was normal. He had gotten some Valium in preparation for the taxi ride back to his nursing home, I learned, so I let him be. He would be back sooner or later.

It was the end of the week, and there were twenty-five empty beds in the hospital. Alice was thrilled because the hospital could come off Catch and Release and would likely stay off through the weekend. She walked to the patient board in the ED and turned the card for Admissions to green, then walked back to the ED office to fetch her white coat and stethoscope. Elaine Cook, the cantankerous smoker, was back in the ED, and Alice wrote her name on the whiteboard next to hers. After she saw her, maybe she would even have the time to teach the medical students for a little while. What a pleasure it was to be a doctor again, without worrying about when the operating room would open up, or whether there were any positive beds.

"Hi Elaine," she said. "What's happening?"

"Same fucking thing." Elaine was puffing away on a nebulizer. Alice put on her stethoscope; Elaine's lungs were a little wheezy, but not worse than usual.

"Any cough or fever?"

"I ran out of my damn inhalers."

"Sorry to hear that," Alice said. "We'll get you another. Are you still smoking?"

"Fuck."

Alice thought Elaine looked about the same as usual, and definitely better than last time. And she smelled like she had been drinking.

"Anything else you need?" Alice asked.

"I don't think so," Elaine said. By the time the replacement inhaler came up from the pharmacy, she had put on her coat and was ready to go.

"See you next time."

"Thank you," she said.

"Think about quitting smoking," Alice said.

"It's not going to happen."

Burnout

When the ED floodgates officially opened again for business, the numbers on my service began to creep northward. One Monday morning, I inherited eight patients already in-house, and four more came by noon. Among the new patients was an eighty-one-year-old man named Howard Short, whose neighbors had called 911 on him, and he was livid. Deaf to his protests, the ED staff lifted him onto one of the hallway gurneys, cranked up the rails and secured the bars from below. For hours, Short tried to engage each person who walked past his gurney, yelling that it was all one big mix-up and he just needed a ride home.

Eventually an emergency doctor opined that the only thing wrong with Short was generalized weakness due to bad arthritis and a moderately flawed short-term memory, alone not huge problems. But he lived by himself, with no family and few friends to speak of, and he'd already been hospitalized before for the same reasons. Even then his doctors had recommended he go to a nursing home, but he'd talked a good game about getting stronger and hiring a home chore worker. This time I knew he was unlikely to return home again. And thus, he was admitted to Four.

"Just fine, just fine," he said, when I entered the room. He was lying on his back.

"Hi, Mr. Short. Did you sleep well last night?"

"Thank you very much," he said. He noticed my white coat, pulled the bedsheets down over his chest, closed his eyes, and said, "You just go ahead."

"Any chest pain? Stomach pain?"

"Only my knees." His eyes remained closed.

"Have you been out of bed today?"

"Nothing wrong with me!"

"Where are you?"

"Seattle!" he exclaimed.

"I mean the kind of place, the type of place, that you're at."

"Well, I'm at church," he said.

"Right now?"

"Like I said."

"Well, this is Harborview, and you can't go home because they won't take you back," I said. His neighbors had surely told him the same thing, but he didn't seem to remember.

"I just need to get up and go," he said pleasantly, his eyes fixed on the ceiling. "If someone could release me from this bed."

"You're not tied down, Mr. Short."

"I could walk fine if I didn't have these boots on my feet." He had puffy wrappings around his ankles to cover sore spots, where the skin had begun to wear away.

"You'll probably have to go to a rehabilitation facility, somewhere you can get therapy to get stronger."

"I'm eighty-one! I'm not as strong as I used to be, what do you expect? I can't listen to this kind of talk."

"The problem isn't that you're eighty-one. It's that you're not getting enough to eat or drink and you're so weak that you're going to the bathroom in a bucket by the sofa. Your neighbors are going to call 911 just as soon as you get home. Don't you think a little bit of physical therapy, to make you stronger, would make sense?"

"Not in no nursing home," he said, triumphantly.

He seemed so completely unaware of his present situation that I turned, frustrated, and simply made an exit from the room. My knock at Barb's door was answered by a nephrology resident, and I remembered that Barb had been bumped to a new spot, this time near the service elevator on Four. She was sharing the new office with two other social workers, and the work space she'd been given was so small that she herself became a potential fire hazard. The door didn't open more than thirty degrees, blocked by her desk chair.

"Mr. Short," I said.

She sighed and said, "He really has nobody." She was wearing a gold "Harborview Cares" pin on her sweater.

"He claims that he once worked on a plantation in Louisiana. I mean he's old, but is he that old?"

"Did he refuse a nursing facility?"

"He did. Again."

"So we're going to have to ask the courts to appoint him a guardian, and hope the guardian will agree it's in his best interests to be in a facility."

"Does anybody think it would be better to set him on the curb and wait for someone to pick him up?"

"The guardianship proceedings will take several weeks at least," she said.

""He really has no idea where he is. We should bundle him up, put him in an ambulance and tell him he's going home. When he gets to the nursing home, they could welcome him back. He'll never know the difference, and it would save him twenty-five thousand dollars."

"Yeah, no kidding," she said. She reached into her file cabinet and extracted a thick package for me. "You'll need to fill this out for the court."

The situation the next morning looked bleak. At least two of the current patients would be fairly painless discharges, but the overnight resident had admitted two more during the early morning hours, both diabetics with out-of-control blood sugars. One was a 350-pound woman who resembled a pyramid and had an abscess on her abdominal wall. The problem was that she could locate the abscess by touch but could not actually see it, buried as it was under a roll of abdominal fat.

The patient had been transferred to Harborview from a small-town hospital east of the mountains because her doctors hadn't known what else to do for her. The chart listed her insulin dose as 250 units daily, which I assumed at first to be a typographical error, since the typical patient used about thirty to sixty units; two hundred and fifty units would kill most people. But the records from the hometown doctor corroborated the dose, and then the patient did, too, and so I supposed that the uncontrolled diabetes and excessive weight were related, that the infection was an entirely predictable consequence of her particular set of circumstances.

The end result was that she had had an abscess drained in the ED and then had been hospitalized so a nurse could lift her skin fold, remove the bandages, inspect the healing wound, and then tape fresh damp gauze back into place.

"You can leave tomorrow if there's a way to get the dressings changed at home," I said.

The patient said she couldn't manage at home, because she lived alone. I asked her about family members, and she said she didn't want to impose. Frustrated, I said that if she couldn't do it and no one could help, she would have to go to a nursing home until the wound improved, which would take a couple of weeks, maybe longer. Threatening the patient with a nursing home wasn't a very elegant strategy, I knew, and I realized that a nursing home was a ridiculous use of limited resources, but so was the hospital, and I didn't know how else to get into the head of a patient who really seemed to have no interest in getting back to health.

After a long pause, the patient finally said, "Let me ask my sister." I stared at her lying flat on her back, with a pained expression on her face. Her legs were so big that her heels weren't touching the bed. She was going to be difficult to discharge, I felt, even though the abscess had already been fixed, even if the sister ultimately agreed to take her in. Patients who were this sedentary often suffered bad complications that more mobile patients were spared.

I left the room and headed for the other diabetic patient's room, which was down the hallway. Before I reached my destination, a colleague flagged me down to say that Paul Brown, the guy with two feet of intestine, had died.

"But he had gotten a job," I said. He had just begun making his comeback.

"And he was dating again," she said. Paul had died at home, but she didn't have any additional information about what had done him in. We walked into one of the doctors' workrooms and sat for a few minutes, remembering some of the things he said and did, wondering how this could have happened just when he seemed to be as well as he had been in years, just when his life was back on track. I had even kind of liked the guy, I said.

Soon enough, though, I was back on my feet, visiting a retired lawyer across the ward who had arrived at the hospital enveloped in the nearly intolerable odor of rotting flesh, a nauseating stench that itself suggested both diagnosis and treatment. The lawyer had been assigned to a semi-private room, I noted, and mercifully, his roommate was a comatose elderly man with a feeding tube sprouting from his nose. The roommate looked similar to the lawyer, I decided.

"It's going to have to come off," I said.

"I can accept that the toe is gone," he said, pointing at one slim digit that was black as coal, that was crusted over and starting to dry as the infection traveled into the foot. He smiled grimly. "I consider the rest of the foot to be negotiable." The treatment for foot gangrene was amputation below the knee, in two stages, to guarantee that the infection had really been cleared before the leg was sewn closed. I shifted from foot to foot and tried again to explain the urgency of the situation, the idea that a diabetic toe infection could become too much for the body to handle beyond a certain point, regardless of how skilled and aggressive the surgeon was. It was likely the entire lower limb would have to come off, I said, or the infection could spread beyond the point of no return.

A Code Blue was called over the public address system, followed by the sounds of dozens of footsteps dashing down the hall and disappearing in the hallway to the new wing, where a patient had suddenly stopped breathing. The announcement gave the location of the code as the GI suite, where colonoscopies and other procedures to examine the intestinal tract were performed. I remembered that one of my patients had been scheduled for a stomach scope that day, but I didn't know when she'd been scheduled to go. I had spent about ninety seconds seeing her earlier, and she'd been a little bit sleepy, which I had chalked up to the

relatively early hour. The patient herself had said she wasn't
a morning person, had rolled over and pulled the blankets
up after a few of my questions, and because I had thirteen patients still to see, I said I'd come back later to visit.
Then I decided that had the code actually been related to
my patient, the GI nurses would have paged me already. I
reoriented myself to the conversation with the lawyer.

"Again, we'll negotiate the foot," the lawyer said.

"I'm not sure what you mean. It's not a doctor you're
negotiating with here. Infections don't negotiate," I said.

"I mean about cutting off the toe," he said. Exasperated,
I told him he didn't need a surgeon for the dry black toe,
because that toe was dead and would slough off on its own
in a week or two. The reason he needed a surgeon was to
prevent further complications, to prevent spread of his bad
infection.

The lawyer grinned and said, "Now that's a cheerful piece
of news."

The surgeons would need to clean up the *living* part of
the foot, I said, because there was so much infected tissue
and pus. He pointed at the multiple bags of intravenous
antibiotics hanging above the head of his bed.

"Yeah. They're great drugs, and they keep the infection
from spreading temporarily."

My pager went off.

"I gotta go," I said abruptly. I flipped the sheet back over
his black and purple foot, waved my hands under hot water,
and hustled out of the room.

As I ran to the GI suite in the west clinic wing, I tried to
tell myself that I wasn't mad at the lawyer, even though
I obviously was. He'd told me that the diabetes hadn't ever
been a problem before, even though a doctor had tried to

prescribe insulin for him years ago. He'd declined the meds, he said, because he felt fine. *See*, I thought, *you got that wrong.* Maybe if he'd lost ten pounds and taken it upon himself to eat a healthy diet, his diabetes would not have progressed so quickly. If he'd taken insulin and his blood sugars had normalized, he probably wouldn't have been susceptible to such an aggressive infection. But the problem was that he had believed there was no problem.

I hurried through the clinic waiting room, through a door marked, ALARM SOUNDS WHEN DOOR OPENS, and up the hallway to the GI suite. There were about two dozen people clustered around my patient's gurney; a few of the residents had started to leave the scene, which was either a good sign or a really bad sign. I made my way to the bedside, trying to think about what could have gone wrong with this patient, and then I saw that she was moving about actively and jabbering incoherently, which meant she had an airway, was breathing, and probably had a pulse. Her blood pressure was slightly low. One of the nurses confirmed that her pulse was strong.

The GI doctor said, "She stopped breathing when we were in the duodenum." She told me that the patient had probably gotten too much sedative medication.

I said, "Plus the methadone she got this morning for opiate withdrawal, plus the pain medications."

"What are the pain medications for?"

I smiled and said, "Cosmic pain."

By now the patient was breathing well, and the ICU resident wanted to know if he should hang around.

"She should probably be observed for a few hours," I said, meaning the patient should go to the ICU. "The ward nurses won't take her back like this." The ICU resident was not happy about this, since the patient wasn't as sick as everyone else he was looking after. I told him that I would take her back when she was more awake and her blood pressure was normal again.

My pager rang. It was Alice calling to say that my old friend Fred Wirth, the drinker with foot gangrene, was again in the ED and needed to come in-house. He had pneumonia, she said, and would probably benefit from being out of the damp weather. I told her I'd be right over, hung up the phone, and logged onto a computer at the GI suite desk, which showed that Wirth hadn't had any testing done or visited the clinic even once since I discharged him last. *Real progress*, I thought.

I walked over to the ED and found Wirth drinking a soda through a straw in one of the treatment rooms.

"Mr. Wirth," I said, snapping the curtain closed behind me. "I'm Dr. Young."

"Nice to meet you," he said.

"I took care of you the last time you were in the hospital. And some of the other times, too."

"Right," he said, nodding sagely.

"We're going to put you in the hospital for a couple of days and give you antibiotics for the pneumonia."

"Sounds fine to me." He took another pull of soda through the straw.

"How come you didn't go to see the doctors in the clinic about your foot?"

He drew back. "I don't remember," he said.

"You were supposed to have a bone scan, to see what's happened with that infection in your foot."

"I guess I forgot."

"I see," I said. I snapped my stethoscope out of my pocket and took a cursory listen to his heart and lungs; there was a little fluid on his lung, probably what Alice was calling pneumonia. His toe had all but come off, and then I noticed white worms moving in his shin ulcer. There was bile in my mouth, and I pulled his pant leg back down quickly before asking how much he was drinking.

"About a fifth," he said.

"Of what?"

"Of whatever I can get."

"Did you have seizures last time you withdrew?"

"I have a high tolerance for Librium."

"When was the last time you took your medications?" He looked puzzled. "For your heart," I said.

"Last week," he said.

I washed my hands and left the room because if I stayed another minute, it was possible that I would strangle him or that I would throw up. It didn't matter what I asked him to do or what I said. He never listened, and I didn't have any way to get through to him. What could I really do for him? He was just going to keep coming back to the hospital for the same damn things every few weeks, and now he had maggots.

I slipped out and headed back to the Fishbowl, staked out a position near one of the computers, and wrote admitting orders. I wondered why couldn't we just cure him once and for all, and not necessarily for his own good, since he never remembered anything that happened to him. It would be for the good of the system: without definitive treatment, he'd come back with a systemic infection and out-of-control diabetes, needing amputation of his entire leg. That would be a hefty expense for Harborview and therefore for everybody else—the patients and the physicians who contributed unwittingly toward his medical care. It was a miracle Wirth hadn't died, but he was just fifty-one years old, so there was no telling how long he might hang on.

In the Fishbowl, I answered a page from the orthopedic surgeon, John Stockman, who proclaimed that the general surgeons should be the ones to take my lawyer to the OR. I told him that one of the general surgeons, Ron Schwarz, had said to me earlier in the day that Stockman should do the procedure. But Stockman said that he and Schwarz had worked it out, so I hung up and paged Schwarz. Schwarz called me back and before I could say anything, he said he'd talked with Stockman, and there was no clear hospital policy about which team was supposed to do foot amputations. Schwarz said he would personally do the procedure as a favor to me if I would continue to take care of the patient afterward.

"Thank you," I said. "Since I don't do surgery." I refrained from commenting on how he would also be doing the *patient* a favor. Instead, I asked when he thought he could operate, and then I shut my mouth, because I did not want to say anything else to alter the surgeon's charitable frame of mind.

"Tomorrow, so long as he doesn't get bumped," he said. He meant that if the hospital got killed with trauma overnight, emergency cases could potentially displace the lawyer from the operative schedule, even though his foot urgently needed debridement. I thanked him as nicely as I could, then hung up and searched the ED for Alice, who was in one of the resuscitation suites, wearing scrubs and a colorful lead apron. She was directing a room full of residents and nurses in a loud, calm voice. The patient had been the restrained passenger in a high-speed T-bone car accident, and a small pool of blood had accumulated beneath the stretcher. She waved smoothly to me in between requests for various medications and fluids, and then she turned and glanced at the monitor, which showed a heart rate of 180. This was definitely not the time to complain about my woes.

A tech in scrubs rolled a portable X-ray machine into the room, and the ED staff backed away from the gurney—six feet was the recommended distance from the radiation source. Alice made her way to the door of the suite to say hello to me. She said she thought that the patient would survive to the operating room, which did not sound like a very good prognosis at all, but Alice looked energized and excited. A nurse thrust an electrocardiogram into Alice's hand. She scanned it quickly, as though she were reading a gossip magazine. I put my hands on my hips and watched the tech shoot the X-rays.

My pager rang: this time it was Barb telling me that the 350-pound patient had convinced her sister to perform nursing duties. The hitch—of course there was a hitch—was that her sister worked two jobs and had four kids and so couldn't get to Seattle until the weekend, which was still three days away. Barb had done her best to find a way around the issue, but the patient had said that on account of her weight, she would be too weak to walk up the stairs of a Greyhound bus.

"So she'll have to stay," Barb said.

"And she'll sit in bed all week and by the weekend be too weak to get up and fix herself something to eat, and all that," I said, and added, "I'm having a bad day."

Barb clucked, and said, "Kid, sometimes that's how it goes." My pager rang yet again, this time to an outside number I didn't recognize. I dropped my pen, hung up with Barb, tossed the pieces of my pager on the Fishbowl counter, and dialed the number.

"Medical examiner."

"You paged?"

"Yes, Dr. Young? We have your patient, Marv Hooley. He was found dead in his hotel room this morning." Marv was the alcoholic whom we'd diagnosed with pleural tuberculosis.

I sighed. "What happened?"

"No evidence of foul play. Looks like natural causes." *Natural causes?*

I said, "I saw him once, a long time ago. But you're looking for his primary care doctor."

"You were the last to see him."

I pulled up Hooley's computer record. The tab listing his primary care doctor read: NONE, and the computer chart indicated I had been last to see him at Harborview. I stared at the screen and thought about what Marv had suffered, including a compromised heart, difficult breathing, loneliness, inclement weather, bitter antibiotics. Probably he died from something that an internist would have known how to treat. Why didn't he go to the clinic? Maybe because it wasn't easy to get into the clinic. There weren't enough internists or family doctors at Harborview or elsewhere in the city to meet the demand, and there was unlikely to be a real expansion in the supply, since primary care was a money-losing proposition for those who weren't seeing a patient every ten minutes. The inadequate numbers of primary care doctors in Seattle meant that at Harborview there was stiff competition for a limited number of spots; you had to be a "good" patient to be retained by the system. You had to show up on time, even though your transportation was unreliable, and then you had to wait hours for a provider to see you. You had to come to appointments with a series of different providers until the system decided you were worthy of a real live primary care doctor, someone you could see every time you came in. I should have known that the system would be perplexing to Marv. He'd shown himself to be a great guy, but not a "good" patient.

"Where are you?" The voice said it could bring the death certificate to me right away for a signature.

"Well," I said. "I'm leaving the ER now, but I'm headed to Three and then to Four. Maybe I can come to you? It's not a problem to make a detour." It wasn't a good idea to sit around waiting in the ER. Copass could walk in anytime and see that you weren't doing anything, and I wanted to avoid that scenario.

The medical examiner's office was on the ground floor of the hospital. To get there I had to leave the hospital and find the examiner's separate entrance, wave through the locked glass door, and get buzzed in. The folder was sitting at the reception desk when I came in, and a friendly bearded man came out to meet me.

"Do you want to see the body?" he asked me.

"I guess I should," I said.

We walked through the corridors and upstairs through the autopsy suite. "We just had a terrible case," the man said. "Fifteen-year-old. Handgun suicide. Gun was a birthday present from his dad." I stared at a chart showing a series of bullet fragments. There were no bodies in sight.

"This way," he said, and led me into a small room. The sheet came off Marv's gray face, and all I could think about was how tall he was.

"I'll sign it," I said, opening the folder.

That night I sat at my dining room table, turned on my laptop, and spat out twelve hundred words about Marv. I typed so fast and loud that my husband called over to ask if everything was all right.

"Fine," I said. "Perfect."

I was still feeling pretty worked up when I got into bed, and I said, "I'm quitting my job."

My husband looked up from his book. It wasn't the first time he'd heard me say something like this, and he replied calmly, "Why don't you wait until morning to decide?"

I said, "I know. I know. I know. I just need to get away from that place for a little while."

A Night Out

During my week off, my friend Robin telephoned to ask if I was interested in joining him at a pharmaceutical dinner that evening at Hinge, a surf and turf restaurant in the fashionable Belltown neighborhood. I hadn't been to a drug dinner since the beginning of my internship, some years earlier, when I'd attended two dinners that involved bottomless libations, passed hors d'oeuvres, and an enormous personal platter of steak and shrimp.

The first had involved an impeccably dressed physician talking up a $2 pill for toenail fungus, which had to be taken every day for three to six months; some patients required a longer course. A doctor in the audience had protested the cost, prompting the speaker to wring his hands and say, "Come on, people. Your patients are spending sixteen bucks a pop for a CD! Let's talk priorities here!" The second event had been a pitch for a stomach drug that was pulled off the shelves shortly thereafter, because patients were dropping dead from arrhythmias linked to the medication.

Robin said that Peter Solomon [not his real name] was speaking. Solomon, an infectious disease doctor at Harborview, had mentored Robin during residency training, and he was widely admired as a clinician and teacher.

My husband was out of town that day, and the idea of getting dressed up and eating at a trendy restaurant on someone else's dime was starting to sound pretty fun so I said, "Why not?" We decided we'd meet at the restaurant, and in a little while I was navigating the streets of Belltown, where the pedestrians were impossibly slim and the dogs were petite and coiffed. I circled the block a few times before a street parking spot opened.

Hinge was dark inside and pulsating with house music. The hostess led me downstairs, through a set of French doors, and into a private room, where the carpeting, wallpaper, and drapes had all been done in a sumptuous red. Jazz hummed softly. About two dozen doctors and a couple of pharmaceutical representatives were gathered in small clusters. A rep strode over, greeted me by name, and apologized that I'd missed the hors d'oeuvres. Could she order me a cocktail?

I said, "Sure. Parking is terrible in this neighborhood." It was a little creepy that the rep knew my name.

She made a pout with her lips, narrowed her eyes, and said, "Oh, you should have done valet! We like to pick that up for you." She helped me out of my coat. Her eyes were the color of emeralds, and she had silky dark hair.

"Yes, that did not occur to me."

"I'll get that drink pronto," she said.

Robin approached and said, "You *made* it!" He was drinking a martini with a lemon twist, and he turned to bat his eyelashes at the drug rep, who flagged down a waiter, then positioned herself in his direction. We were seated a few minutes later. The menu featured a salad followed by a platter of grilled shrimp and New York strip. The only decision to make was how the steak should be cooked. I ordered mine rare.

Solomon wore a sportcoat and slacks, and he walked assuredly to the front of the room after an introduction from the rep and launched into his talk about pneumonia. I looked around. Most in attendance were probably twenty years older than me, and everyone seemed riveted by the presentation. The main course arrived, and Solomon began to discuss different clinical scenarios and the infectious disease society antibiotic guidelines to match these situations.

Soon I was distracted with my shrimp, which I was trying to eat gracefully with my fingers. The shrimp were salty and chewy, and as I ate I thought about how drug dinners had been a fixture of physician culture for as long as I had known, that I and many of my colleagues intermittently attended the events. I poked at my overcooked steak and thought about the cost of dinner—$50? More? The drug company would pick up the check, log the evening as a marketing or development expense, and recoup the cost the following month in sales. The people who were really paying for dinner were those purchasing the drugs I was now supposed to recommend.

I wondered how I could still justify the evening to myself, and I decided that I was just cheap; I had been lured in with $50 steak. I could hear Solomon lecture at Harborview anytime and he would give the same talk nearly verbatim; I didn't have to accept an expensive meal in order to learn from his wisdom. The value of my attending the dinner to the consumer—the patient—seemed somewhat dubious. The medications often featured at these events were generally the newest and priciest drugs, ones that most patients could hardly pay for out of pocket, and the clinical record was not generally strong at that early date. Some of the drugs would inevitably be pulled from shelves or acquire black box warnings in the years to come, as the evidence for damaging side effects mounted.

The industry's efforts to sell drugs had been highly successful, in any case, and growing medication costs had driven double-digit increases in health care spending in the 1990s and early 2000s (hospital care became the largest spending stimulus in 2005). Harborview had several medications that could be used only with retroactive approval from Scott Barnhart, because they were so prohibitively expensive. One was an intravenous medication called Xigris, or recombinant human activated protein C, which the hospital purchased for use in cases of severe septic shock, at a cost of $10,153 for the five-day course. There was also recombinant factor VIIa, used in life-threatening bleeding at a cost of $4,608 per dose.

The prices were stunning, but in reality, they reflected an aggressive change in industry-wide pricing models. Prices no longer really reflected development and manufacturing costs so much as they were derived from complicated models that predicted the point of maximal return. As a result, newer antibiotics were selling for $55 per pill while providing only slight advantage over established medications that might retail at 25 cents per pill. These exorbitant prices were likely one of the factors that had led to Harborview's decision to ban drug reps from the dozens of teaching conferences at the hospital every week. In previous years, there had been more of a symbiosis, and the reps had brought lunch on a daily basis.

And the value of new drugs did not always seem to measure up to the price. Dave French, for example, had received the first twenty-four hours of his ten-grand infusion in the ICU before he began to ooze blood from every orifice—a known side-effect of recombinant activated protein C—and it was doubtful that the drug had contributed in any meaningful way to his recovery. The $55 antibiotic, as another example, treated highly resistant bacteria that we sometimes saw in homeless patients, who were exposed in shelters where they lived in close proximity with others.

These expensive drugs didn't necessarily make people healthier, but relentless drug advertising and marketing—fueled by one-third of drug company profits—had conditioned us to believe that we needed medications for better living, that the new drugs really improved our quality of life. It was as though we'd given up on the idea that real health was attainable. And it was not just Harborview patients who suffered from this way of thinking. Tens of thousands of people developed avoidable diseases every year like diabetes, high blood pressure, stroke, heart disease, and obesity, and immediately turned to drug remedies. Standard care for someone with heart disease and no symptoms, for example, typically called for a minimum of four drugs.

I emerged from my fog as Solomon wrapped up his lecture. Later he would tell me that he rarely did the talks anymore because many companies insisted that the talks focus on a specific drug, and some even required that speakers use company-prepared slides. He only spoke at events in which he controlled the content, he told me, and he'd put his wife and two children through school with the fees he'd earned. I didn't know exactly what to make of this. I trusted Solomon, but I wondered just how sophisticated I was in recognizing the more subtle forms of commercial persuasion. It just didn't seem that drug dinners could be an unbiased source of medical education.

Now the waitstaff descended with trays of chocolate mousse, and I sampled a few spoonfuls while Solomon responded deftly to the audience queries. Robin had slipped to the back of the room to whisper with the green-eyed drug rep and when he returned, we snatched our coats and headed out the door. In a moment we were on the street, where life became fresh again. In my hand I carried a small white box with my leftover steak and potatoes, which was practically enough for a full meal. A moment later I passed the box to an older man sitting on the street and then headed home.

Diversion

The day before I was supposed to visit Dave French, the drug addict who'd turned clean, he called me in a panic.

"I can't make it at home!" he shouted. I had to hold the phone a few inches from my ear because of his yelling. "I need to have my morphine increased! I need to go to a nursing home where I can get three square meals a day! I'm going to come down to Harborview and tell them I talked to you and get admitted to the hospital."

"Who's your doctor out there?"

"I'm just not making it! I need to come to Harborview!"

"Someone will see you anytime, and you can say you talked to me. But I can't promise they'll admit you to the hospital. It depends what they find out."

He sighed, then said, "Gotta go," and hung up. A week later he called to say he was feeling much better, that his doctor had increased his morphine, and that he'd stayed home after all. He wondered when I was going to visit, so I told him I'd drive out to see him on my next week off. Almost two years had elapsed since his hospitalization in the ICU, and he made a point of telling me over the phone that he'd remained clean and sober.

When I arrived, he was leaning on a second-floor balcony railing smoking a cigarette. He lived in a two-story walk-up apartment in rural Washington State, up the street from the local police department and public high school ("Home of the Trojans"). Two hundred yards from his front door was the new cement frame of a shopping center, surrounded by backhoes busily moving earth. He waved me up and moved stiffly into the apartment, which was outfitted with aging shag carpet and wood veneer panels.

Dave poured me a mug of strong black coffee and we sat in the living room, which held two couches arranged at right angles and a large wooden coffee table. He said, "My father was one of the finest men I have ever known."

His mother, on the other hand, typically started her day with a highball and was sometimes passed out on the floor, naked, when he and his brother returned from school. The brothers would drag her to bed and cover her with blankets. "He was the better of the two parents," Dave said. "He put Mom in treatment between forty and sixty times." His parents had divorced when he was thirteen, he said, and his father, Sam, won custody of the kids.

But Sam was generally absent from the family's domestic life, engaged as he was with his wholesaling business, and Dave remembers craving paternal attention. He started dropping acid regularly, and his grade average plunged. He experimented with mescaline, peyote, mushrooms, and cocaine. "You could buy a pink Baskin-Robbins tasting spoon packed with cocaine for $50 in the high school parking lot," he said. "My drug use was the family secret. Nobody knew what to do, and we were too embarrassed to talk about it."

Out of high school, Dave was drafted for Vietnam. His first tainted urinalysis was at three weeks. He was dishonorably discharged after he flunked a second test a month later, so he returned home and became the youngest manager at the Nordstrom department store, only to lose that job when he disappeared on a bender. He got his girlfriend pregnant and married her, but they split months after his son Tyler was born. He worked as a prison guard and injected heroin with prisoners on the sly. He was fired from a cushy public transit position when a urinalysis revealed methadone. He stopped paying child support; his ex-wife moved in with a stand-up comic and had his visitation rights suspended.

Not long afterward, his mother swallowed a handful of Valium and Ritalin that a doctor had prescribed for alcoholism. She fell and struck her head, sustaining nothing more than "a little cut," Dave said. He put her to bed and covered her, and she died later that night of bleeding in her brain. But he never connected her alcoholism and prescription drug abuse with his addiction.

By age forty, Dave was sleeping under bridges or in his car, cashiering at a thrift store, and doing cocaine two or three times a day. His life revolved around the feeling of completeness he had when walking around with drugs in his pocket. Dave called or visited his father only to ask for money, claiming that he needed cigarettes or a car part. Sam never gave more than $40 at a time, trying to minimize the harm the money might do.

At age forty-eight, Dave was arrested for drug possession. He told the judge that jail would do nothing for him—getting drugs in jail was a cinch, he knew—so the judge shipped him off to intensive drug treatment. He stayed clean for ten days afterward, used cocaine once, and collapsed while walking across a parking lot. He had just withdrawn cash to pay off a friend, he remembered the cement coming up at his face, and that was it. He didn't recall missing Thanksgiving dinner because of the flu. He didn't remember chest pains, difficulty breathing, or any other suggestion that he might be ill.

He said, "I recall people behind my bed doing drugs. I was at the division of Harborview in Ballard."

"There is no division of Harborview in Ballard."

"I didn't recognize my sisters for a while," he said. "I experienced the kindling effect. If you stop using cocaine for a time and then pick it up again, one-fiftieth of a gram can make your aorta explode."

"Something like that."

"I lost a tooth," he said, showing me the gap in his bottom teeth. "Any idea where that went?"

I shook my head. "Maybe it got knocked out when they put the tube in your throat to keep you breathing. You were sick. We didn't know if you would make it."

What he was certain of was that Sam was standing at the foot of his bed after the ventilator tubing was pulled from his windpipe, and that the fictions and shadows of his life all fell away at that moment. It was a miracle, he said, but his family took him in after several months of painful physical rehabilitation. The consensus was that he should live far from Seattle, where drugs were temptingly easy to access, so he took up residence in his sister's home, and later moved into his own apartment.

Dave returned to his father's story. Some months earlier, Sam had died of complications of congestive heart failure. His father was a strong man, Dave said. He was a man who could will himself to stop drinking, who quit smoking on his first try and climbed Mount Rainier just to show that he could do it. Fifteen years earlier, Sam had beaten colon cancer, and Dave thought he would beat the heart failure too.

"He was trying to show me how to do it," Dave said.

On the last day of his father's life, Dave presented him with a coin marking one year of sobriety from drugs and alcohol, his longest period of sobriety since childhood. His father had rubbed the coin with his fingers.

"I think he finally believed there was a chance. I wanted him to know I was as strong as he was," Dave said. Sometimes he had intensely real dreams that his father was sitting on the living room sofa reassuring him about the future, and he cried when he woke up and the warmth left him.

In his will, Sam left Dave a comfortable inheritance, which he would receive as a monthly allowance—so he wouldn't be tempted to blow everything on dope—after his stepmother died. After Dave died, the remainder of the money would go to the Salvation Army.

Dave hadn't seen his son, Tyler, since hospitalization, but he knew that Tyler had been dishonorably discharged from the military for continuing drug use. He'd been to treatment five times already, Dave said, and in jail once. Dave told me that Tyler had saved his life, and he was incredibly grateful to him. He wanted Tyler to come live with him in rural Washington, to start a new life thousands of miles from his addicted buddies, but Tyler had thus far declined. Dave shrugged and told me, "He has to go through what he has to go through. Recovery has to be in your heart." It was a phrase I knew he'd verbalized hundreds of times at Narcotics Anonymous meetings, and over and over while he meditated at home. Still, he continued to pay his phone bill, hoping that one day Tyler would call and say he was coming home.

It was sunny and breezy on the drive back to Seattle, and I thought about how Dave French's story ought to end right there, as a happy tale of recovery and redemption: a lifelong drug addict nearly dies, comes to recognize his ability to self-destruct, and is transformed. He kicks his addictions, reconciles with his estranged father, and, as his father is dying, gives him his one-year sobriety coin to take to the grave, which convinces the father, on his deathbed, that the son is finally living a life of strength. Dave's story even left a bit of mystery to chew on, the uncertainty about whether Tyler would come around. The amazing thing about the story was that it was actually true—wondrously true.

The less pleasant postscript was that, in his new life, Dave depended entirely on prescription drugs for his well-being. "It's hell without the meds," he said to me. He used antipsychotic and anxiolytic drugs to take the edge off the flashbacks and nightmares that he suffered as a result of dropping acid in his twenties. He needed twice-daily slow-release morphine to stay ahead of disabling leg pains, and his doctor had to gradually increase the dose so that the morphine alone ate 30 percent of his monthly allowance. But Dave paid for the morphine out of pocket, because otherwise he'd be unable to walk at all. I remembered what Sam had said during Dave's hospitalization, when he'd described Dave as an unhappy social misfit, and I thought I understood where Sam had been coming from.

When I revisited that time, I didn't regret my role in keeping Dave alive, even though the new life that he lived was filled with terrible physical pain. I didn't think there really had been a right thing to do with Dave in the ICU. The more I learned about him and his father, the more complex the choices seemed, even with the benefit of so much hindsight. If Dave really didn't want to live, he'd take an easy and fast route, meaning he'd go on a big drug junket and end it all. But he'd had a couple of years and hadn't pulled the trigger yet.

I thought about the decision to keep Dave alive, and I knew that one reason we persevered was that Sam had seemed like a rich jerk who wanted nothing more than to put his troubled son away for good. But Sam wasn't the sort of person to reveal his disfigured private life, the backstory of a first wife and a second son, two people he loved as much as anyone else in the world, who pitched about for decades under the influence of booze and drugs, resistant to his coaxing, to the support he'd offered time and time again.

Sam knew his son was spiraling toward an early death, saw his grandson headed down the same road, and came to call the outcome inevitable. Maybe his wish to let Dave go in the ICU was his aging bleat of powerlessness, his admission of how genuinely difficult it is to help another human being.

Bring It On

On the last night of my week off, I went to hear Kermit Jackson play his horn. I was determined to get back into the swing of things, determined to face the coming week. The club was crowded, and I had to park a quarter-mile up the strip. Ten minutes later, seated at a stage-side table, I realized that I'd come for an open mike night, that Kermit wasn't giving a show of his own. Still, I ordered a beer and settled in.

The first act was a woman wearing sequins and heavy stage makeup. She sang off-key covers, and following her was a ponytailed kid who strummed an acoustic guitar, and then an accordionist who was also not terribly good, but for whom the crowd clapped wildly. I scanned the room every few minutes, checking for Kermit, wondering if he would light up the room when he appeared on stage or if he might come off about the same as everyone else. I hoped he would knock everybody's socks off.

I turned to the window and watched the ferryboats coming into harbor in Seattle. At ten o'clock there was still no sign of Kermit, so I finished nursing my beer and decided that he was not going to make it tonight, that his home had to have a curfew. When the acts switched again, I darted for the cashier and then headed for the door. By the time I got to my car, I was laughing out loud. A semi-psychotic patient had just stood me up. *What a turkey*, I thought.

A few days later I ran into Pat Fleet, Kermit's primary doctor, in the hallway between the hospital wards and the clinics. Fleet was clutching size 13 leather sandals destined for the feet of a patient who had been agitating for a referral to see Sig Hansen, the premier foot surgeon. They looked like something that Fleet himself would wear.

Fleet grinned and said, "He needs to stop wearing those skinny pimp shoes. He needs a bigger toebox." He said that he had found the shoes at Goodwill, and that he'd also been lucky enough to find a pair of pants that fit him perfectly. "You never know," he said.

I reported my attempt to see Kermit perform at the club. Fleet smiled broadly and said, "Agent K. Have you heard him play?"

"No such luck," I said. Fleet said that Kermit sometimes played on the ward when he had his horn, and one of the long-time nurses on Three had played gigs with him. I mentioned that Kermit had tried to sell me his CD, but that I hadn't had any cash on me. Fleet offered to burn me a copy if he could get his computer into the right frame of mind. I stared after him as he walked away, turned left, and disappeared down the hallway that lead to the clinics. *He is one of the true heroes of Harborview*, I thought. He'd spent his entire life taking on patients he described as "some really cultural people," patients who were a menace to their doctors, patients who scammed and manipulated and broke the resolve of everyone who came before. I had no idea how Fleet had weathered the grind for nearly forty years, and I decided that it was time to ask him.

Fleet's office was about the size of a large walk-in closet and was located behind an unmarked door on Ten in the original hospital building, in the gray zone between the division of nephrology and the division of pulmonary and critical care. I studied the office address posted above the doorframe, knocked, and he hollered that I should let myself in. He was leaning back in his desk chair when I entered, and talked gruffly into the telephone about a patient's narcotics. There was a narrow path that led from the office door to the desk, and on either side of the path, taller than me, were stacks of books and journals, as well as some file cabinets labeled with yellowing tabs that looked like they'd been handmade with a real typewriter about forty years earlier.

He gestured for me to sit down in an old wooden chair that faced the desk, and while I waited for him to get off the phone, I studied the thousands of items strewn about the place. In addition to a great deal of printed matter, there was a stack of folded clothes, a few framed photographs of his children and grandchildren, a recipe for Brazilian feijoada, and dozens of orange prescription vials full of pills, which I soon learned were medications that his patients had cast off for one reason or another, and which he planned to bring to Nicaragua, where he volunteered a couple of times every year. Fleet finished his conversation, replaced the handset, turned to me, and crossed his arms.

First, I said, I wanted to settle the matter of whether or not he'd invented WD-40, the ubiquitous substance sold in every drugstore and hardware outfit in America. Fleet's name had been linked with WD-40 all of the years I had been at Harborview, and among house staff the idea had taken on the proportions of urban legend. Some speculated that Fleet went to great lengths to disguise himself as a down-market nephrologist who rode the bus to work like everybody else.

Fleet gestured with his arms and empathetically denied that he had invented anything.

"I was working for the Navy in a lab in San Diego, and what basically happened was that I couldn't follow the directions." He explained that WD stood for wax density, and told me that rather than adding wax density 15, as he had been instructed to, he had added wax density 40, by mistake. His mistake had worked spectacularly.

"So you invented WD-40," I said.

"You can't invent something that already exists," he replied, shrugging. "I discovered that WD-40 was useful. I didn't get a dime for it."

That was pretty representative of the way Fleet talked about himself for the following two and a half hours. He was warm, funny, and entertaining, but he spun himself as someone who bumbled through life, in a way that almost seemed deliberate, and no matter how I asked the questions, he seemed unable to put in words what made him tick.

The way he put it to me, specifically, was, "I never had much of a plan." He grew up in Southern California and became a tuna fisherman during his teenage years, a career path that was foiled, he said, by his mistake of winning a scholarship to St. Mary's College in northern California. He made up his mind to forgo college until his father, a career serviceman with the merchant marines, prevailed upon him. Still, Fleet arrived at St. Mary's a couple of weeks late because his fishing boat didn't come back in time. He enrolled in a full schedule, and then failed to make it to many of his classes, except for his physics and great books sections.

Fleet had no lifelong convictions about entering medicine, no formal *goals*; he only knew that he wanted to play professional baseball. He could hit and catch well, and he signed on to play with the Pennsylvania league. After one season, he recognized he would never make the majors on account of his throwing arm, which he had injured in a childhood bicycling accident. The minor league traveling life didn't interest him very much anyway, and because all of his college buddies were applying to medical school, he decided that he would, too. He applied to Creighton, in Nebraska, owing to its reputation at that time for taking everyone, and he was accepted.

Fleet moved to Omaha and talked himself into free room and board at the Veteran's Administration Hospital by offering to look after the radiology department's nuclear reactor, which had just been purchased for the new section of nuclear medicine. His hoax wasn't discovered until his senior year, which meant that he had lived and eaten for free for most of his medical school career. He smiled, and then said the first transparent thing of the morning: "I loved medical school. I loved being a resident. I loved being a fellow." He told me that he chose nephrology because of a medical school professor who'd taught his kidney course.

"One day I told him that nobody understood what the hell he was talking about, and the professor responded, 'That's how nephrology is,'" Fleet said. The idea of conquering a specialty nobody understood was just the sort of challenge that appealed to Fleet. He came to Seattle for internal medicine training, elected fellowship training in nephrology, and afterward chose to work at Harborview because he admired a brilliant young attending named Marvin Turck, an infectious disease specialist who was also a popular teacher.

Why did he like Harborview so much? "I like to figure out how things work and then fix them," he told me. But surely it went deeper than that, I urged. "I like applying my knowledge to people," he continued.

Had he ever considered private practice? No, he said, waving off the idea. He'd always been happy at Harborview.

His children had grown up around the hospital, he said, because there hadn't been child care back then, and he added, "My kids never wanted to end up like me, because I spent too much time at work." This seemed somewhat disingenuous, since two of the four children from his first marriage had become doctors. Both had hewn fairly closely to the path he'd taken; one had done internal medicine residency in Seattle, just like he had, and the other had come home to do a nephrology fellowship at the University of Washington, also as he had done. She had been at the hospital for several months during my first year as an attending.

But nothing, it seemed, could deter Fleet from his idea that he was the antihero of Harborview. When I asked him to describe his patients, he said they were "people who are just awful." They were often abusive and threatening, and when I asked why he took them on he shrugged, "Well, they just show up. I don't invite them." He tried to give his patients industry-standard health care, he said. He tried to treat them fairly and listen to their vision for how things ought to go. He never threatened consequences, but he also didn't negotiate.

"Nobody's behavior has made it impossible for me to take care of them." He had no idea how many patients identified him as their primary doctor—how many patients, in other words, that he had in his clinic "panel." The number, I suggested, was likely in the thousands, but he was unwilling to venture a guess. He said he'd never closed his panel or kicked anybody out, which was what most other doctors did when they became too busy or couldn't take it anymore. "I'm not really sure what a panel is," he said, waving his hands.

I knew that Fleet's patients were generally very loyal to him. In my opinion, it was because he offered a full-service approach to medical care, because he was available to help out whenever a patient needed something, even if the problem was something like acid reflux or knee pain, something that most specialists would condescend to pass back to the patient's primary care doctor. Fleet even drew blood in the clinic if he thought it could save the patient a wait at the laboratory.

Fleet appeared to have no problem with being a de facto primary care doctor, an old-fashioned GP for most of his patients, in spite of his training as a specialist. This was part of the reason I thought of him as the consummate doctor, I realized, because he always tried to do what served the patient best. He saw whoever showed up when he was in the clinic, even if the patient didn't have an appointment. Of course, this meant that his clinic days were absolute chaos. He relied heavily on his able RN, Patty, who made sure that his patients were well cared for, and who otherwise ran interference for him.

It was here in the clinic, I surmised, where my idea of Fleet as the ideal doctor clashed with the most contemporary iteration of Harborview. On most of his clinic days, his front desk staff would register drop-in patients until the computer froze at the twelve-patient limit for a half-day session. Of course, twelve was far below the usual number he generally saw during that time window, and when the computer froze, the algorithm called for patients to make an appointment for another day and time, or to present themselves to the emergency department. Fleet didn't think the system made very much sense, and he found it ludicrous that a patient couldn't see his regular doctor because a computer didn't understand how to bill more than twelve patients in a three-and-a-half-hour period.

Fleet told me that although he had always loved being at Harborview, his job had become less fun in recent years with the new documentation requirements, with the administrative roadblocks that came between him and the care of his patients. He would put his patients in an exam room anyway, even after the computer froze at twelve. The only time a problem arose was when he wanted an X-ray, and that was because the system required X-ray order forms to be labeled with computer-generated patient stickers. Naturally, the system couldn't print stickers for patients who weren't registered.

Later, Fleet told me that the public relations department had consulted him years back on a newfangled logo for the hospital, a blue-green design that showed off the original building's art deco style. That didn't capture the place at all, he told the public relations people. If you wanted to represent the hospital, you had to show a guy lying in a gutter in Pioneer Square, and out of the corner of that guy's eye, shining up on the hillside, would be Harborview. That idea captured Fleet in a nutshell.

When I returned to the service, the diabetic lawyer had his second procedure and came out of the OR singing the hospital's praises. By the time I got to the recovery room, in the basement, his anesthesia had worn off completely. "You people run a first-class outfit," he said to me, with the reverence of the converted. The poison was gone from his blood, he said, and added, "Everyone here is a total professional. Thank you." A few days later, he was measured for a prosthetic leg. He took it like he was being fitted for a baseball uniform.

In all, the ward service had loosened considerably. The woman who'd coded in the GI suite was back on her feet and swearing at the nurses; she was quickly returned to the women's shelter. The pyramid-shaped woman with diabetes left with her sister some eight epic days after she'd arrived. Fred Wirth, the drinker with maggots, left one afternoon and never returned, for his belongings or his medications, and eventually air traffic gave his bed to a patient waiting in the ED. The only one left on the wards was eighty-nine-year-old Howard Short, who was going on hospital day number fifteen, and the word was that his guardianship proceedings would be delayed for another month and a half because of a big trial that was starting. Short spent his days lying in bed, and despite the nurses' pleas, he refused to get up. "Why do I need to?" he asked me. "I'm eighty-one." So I tried again: "If you don't get up, you can't go back to your apartment, so we'll have to find you to a place where you can live for the rest of your life."

"Hell no," he said.

"Okay," I said, laughing. "Anything you need right now?"

"How about some apple juice," he said.

"Sure," I said. I went to the pantry, fetched a few juice containers for him from the fridge, and reminded him to ring his call button if he needed anything else.

A few weeks later, I opened the story I'd written about Marv Hooley, the drinker with tuberculosis whose death certificate I had recently signed, and found it to be an incoherent editorial. I worked on it, disguised his identity, and soon the manuscript was flying through the electronic ether and uploaded to a medical journal editor's desk in Chicago.

Some months later the editor emailed comments from the peer reviewer, who disagreed with how I'd interpreted Marv's actions. She (I imagined the reviewer as an over-worked mid-career woman) wrote, "I don't think the system failed him. I think he opted out of this system and all systems, which is his choice." He had to take responsibility for his addiction and ultimately for his health. She asked whether he really slept on a mat, and she concluded, "Don't assume you can put on your cape and rescue a patient who is resistant to the efforts of primary care and substance abuse services."

At first I was amazed. In my mind, Marv's story wasn't intended as the usual doctor-as-hero fare. In my mind, the story was about how the health care system, at least in Seattle, offered little drug and alcohol treatment for people with the wrong kind of funding. It was about having too few primary care doctors to absorb all of Seattle's indigent patients—or about an inadequate paying clientele to fund care for the uninsured. In my mind, the issue really wasn't as much that Marv had rejected his social responsibilities. The issue was that Marv had no money, and there just weren't many options for people with addictions and no money.

My feeling was that Marv had been foiled by what some people said was the greatest medical care in the world. In America, we had carved out medical specialties for every organ system and area of the body, and we'd split most of the specialties between medical and surgical treatment. When we ran out of ways to further divide up diseases, we created new specialties for every clinical setting, including the hospital wards, intensive care unit, emergency room, and nursing home. Does it serve patients well to see a different doctor every time their condition changes a little bit? Or when a different part of the body starts to hurt?

I believed that specialists could offer unique and useful input, but I didn't think that a system driven by specialists served Marv very well. What he seemed to need, in hindsight, was somebody whom he knew and trusted, someone he could find when he wanted help. He needed a primary care doctor that he didn't have to wait two months to see; the EDs were packed with people who, like him, couldn't wait that long. The health care system and its highly trained specialists offered Marv more social disconnectedness, not access.

When I began to work on the story again, I decided that some of the reviewer's comments had merit, and as I wrote my responses I realized that people who would read the story in print would apply moral judgments to Marv and to the medical care I had provided. Some of the judgments, I anticipated, could be pretty harsh. We hold dear a cultural narrative that paints America as a land of opportunity, a place where anyone can work hard and move up in life. We believe in self-reliance and lionize those that rise from rags to riches, like the hard-working ghetto kid who gains admittance to Princeton, like an immigrant who arrives with twenty dollars in hand and launches a successful small business. We believe in pulling ourselves up by our own bootstraps, and we apply this myth to our judgments about poor people. The enduring legislation passed by President Bill Clinton and the 1996 Republican Congress mandated that welfare recipients demonstrate their desire to work or risk losing their public benefits. The suggestion was that those who made something of themselves deserved assistance more.

Perhaps because of these myths, we enjoyed helping a sick patient get well, enjoyed seeing a poor person get ahead and realize the American dream, enjoyed being part of the bootstraps narrative. I was no exception. Taking care of patients like Dave French and Marv felt good. I had gone out of my way for these people, and it seemed possible that I paid more attention to and worked harder for these Horatio Alger types, the ones who were kind to the nurses and weren't looking to game the system. These were patients that many medical practitioners would have been happy to care for, too.

When patients disregarded medical advice, when they appeared not to care about their health and did nothing to advance their cause, as was the case with Fred Wirth, the drinker with maggots, or Mirabelle Fleming, the drug-abusing mother with a seven-year-old in foster care, I quickly grew frustrated. In order to continue taking care of these patients, I had to believe there was little I could do to help, and not blame myself or anyone else for their deaths.

The doctor who had reviewed Marv's story had written in her comments that the practice of "cherry-picking," or selectively providing help, was where a nice story about caring for a poor man falls apart under ethical scrutiny. She was right, even if it was human nature to feel preferences. It was why, in case anyone forgot, Copass had mandated that every ED patient be treated with equal respect and care, no matter how unpleasant the person was, no matter how many times he'd come to the ED for the same damn problem.

The social contract at the county hospital worked like this: patients came because they were sick, and doctors helped because they were able. When a patient improved and was discharged, the relationship dissolved between the patient and doctor, between the patient and society. Providing free medical care was no guarantee of future performance, as the disclaimer goes in so many "investment" businesses. To do things right at Harborview, physicians and nurses and social workers had to view patients as discrete phenomena, as unique individual events, and sometimes had to suspend their moral judgment and just care for the patient. The hospital veterans had learned that such judgments did not help patients get well sooner, did not help patients live with chronic illness or kick unsavory habits. But everyone at Harborview trudged on because they just never knew what would make the difference.

Black Friday

It rained so hard on a Thursday afternoon in December that water fell from the sky in sheets. Hillsides weakened and crumbled onto roads. Streets turned into rivers, carrying away trash and branches. The rain fell harder than it had during the previous month, when flooding washed out homes and river bottomland, swept away farm animals in the eastern reaches of the county, and Seattle set an all-time record for rain.

On Thursday night the sky took on a steel-gray shine and the wind gathered speed, chasing rain clouds east to the mountains, where several feet of resort-quality snow fell. At the airport, the wind reached sixty knots, causing airplanes to veer about wildly as they attempted to land, and across western Washington, trees swayed madly and crashed down on electrical lines. By midnight, a million and a half homes across the region were without power. The temperature dropped to the 30s.

The extent of the damage was not apparent until the sun came up. Trees had fallen on homes, driveways, cars, and roads. Chilly citizens flocked into stores, where the power remained on, and passed the time by shopping for the holidays. A rumor circulated that two suburban gas stations had run out of fuel, because so many people were driving around in order to stay warm. The sky turned pink and hazy with the smoke from wood fires.

As the sun set on Friday evening, patients began to present themselves to the triage desk at the Harborview ED in greater numbers than recalled at any time. People who were unable to fill critical prescriptions due to shuttered pharmacies arrived with symptoms of acute heart failure and with sky-high blood pressure; those who used home oxygen and had been unable to recharge their tanks came with exacerbations of their asthma and emphysema. Ambulances ferried in the sickest of the elderly from cold, dark nursing homes.

Alice was working as the emergency communications director of the day, her last in a stretch before she would fly out for vacation. The first paramedic call reporting a Mass Casualty Incident (MCI) came over the radio at twelve minutes after 7 p.m., from an apartment complex in Kent, twenty miles away, in south King County. Alice scribbled the information down and within minutes had activated the citywide patient triage system. The first decision was to transport all casualties to Harborview, so that families could be kept together—most of the patients would be arriving in separate vehicles—and to streamline coordination with the hyperbaric medicine physician at Virginia Mason Hospital, a few blocks to the north.

Alice called Copass's cell phone. He was on the Olympic Peninsula visiting his grandchildren, but he picked up right away; it seemed that he'd been in contact with key people across the Seattle area for several hours already. One of the nearby nursing homes was without power, owing to a faulty generator, he told Alice, and the nursing home director was thinking about sending its 140 patients to Harborview. Alice described the crowded situation in the ED for him, and they discussed opening the Garden View area for the carbon monoxide cases. Garden View was a bit of hallway between the social work desk and the ambulance ramp that, in crisis situations, could host ten stretchers and laboratory, EKG, and X-ray capabilities, in order to expedite evaluation and treatment of patients.

Copass emphasized that she and the staff would have to stay vigilant about families getting separated, especially with so many children involved. Equally as important, they would have to devise ways of getting the word out to patients' friends and neighbors and relatives about the danger of indoor grills and generators, since those who were susceptible were generally not receiving television or radio news. They were all potential patients with the ability to further overload the city's emergency response system.

Forty-five minutes after the initial MCI alert, the first of the thirty-two patients from the Kent apartment building began to arrive, high-flow oxygen masks pulled tightly against their faces. The patients, most of whom were age twenty or younger, seemed able-bodied and troubled only by an odd sort of confusion. Few spoke English, and they indicated discomfort by pointing at their heads, chests, abdomen, and then at their heads again. The carboxy-hemoglobin levels, drawn and run in the hallway, ranged from the single digits up to the low thirties, suggesting a range of mild to severe carbon monoxide poisoning. In a half hour, the most symptomatic of the first wave of patients were moved to Virginia Mason and admitted to the hospital's hyperbaric chamber, which delivered oxygen at several times atmospheric pressure and displaced carbon monoxide from the blood, a physiological process similar to deep-sea diving. The "dive tank," as medical personnel called it, looked like a segment of an airplane cabin with electric blue carpeting.

Alice returned to the radio room and called her colleague Bob Kalus, who was scheduled to take over ED communications in the morning. They had planned to speak anyway, to discuss the day's important news, and she said, "I think you're going to have to come in." She described the Kent apartment poisonings and said that more were expected, perhaps many more. Bob thought Alice sounded calm, so he finished eating dinner with his wife, who reminded him that Alice was always calm. Bob said that he would go into the hospital for a couple of hours to help out if he could. His wife, who was also a physician, said she might not wait up for him.

Twenty minutes later, Bob walked into the radio room. Alice had a page out to Scott Barnhart, and she thought she might hug Bob, she was so glad to see a familiar face. Scott called back a minute later; he was in Tacoma, thirty-five miles south, dining with friends. She told him they were having some trouble in the ED, that they had seen so many patients and were anticipating many more. There didn't seem to be an end in sight, she said.

She and Bob headed for Garden View, which was bustling like a market bazaar. Several patients occupied each stretcher, and it seemed like a dozen others were milling about and talking in panicky Amharic, Vietnamese, Somali, Tagalog, and Russian. Oxygen tanks had been arranged on racks that resembled Christmas trees, and every patient was attached to one of the tanks by a line of clear plastic tubing. Alice and Bob stopped at each stretcher to examine the patients. It had become a little difficult to keep everybody straight. People kept moving around and many of the patients' names sounded pretty similar. Local interpreters were in short supply, presumably because their cell phones had gone dead and they could not be reached, so much of the initial interpreting went through the youngest patients, who spoke a modicum of English.

Bob's head spun trying to keep straight the laboratory data on the dozens of patients in the hallway and to organize the information into something actionable. Thankfully, many were talking and making sense, and none looked terribly sick. Using hand movements, he pleaded with several patients to stay in place, and he entertained the idea of writing every person's carboxyhemoglobin value on their arm with a Sharpie pen, so that decisions could be made quickly and not forgotten or confused.

Scott Barnhart pulled into Harborview's parking garage after receiving Alice's distress call, apologizing to his friends, and departing hastily for Seattle. On his drive up the interstate, he spoke with the county public health official, describing the situation in the community and at the hospital. The poisonings had the potential to quickly take on epidemic proportions, he said, and he reiterated the concern that many potential victims were difficult to reach.

Scott came in through the west entrance and stopped at the Board in the admitting office. Three phones were ringing at once. The nurses in air traffic control told him they were having a hard time with the more than thirty patients who needed a hospital bed right away, plus the dozen who had gone to the hyperbaric chamber, the two dozen who would be going during the next round—some of whom were related to patients in the first group, and all of whom were presumably returning for observation— and the four hundred other patients already in-house. The last positive bed had been filled much earlier in the day, and now the usual negative bed spaces were full. The cafeteria was being converted into a shelter for patients who required an overnight stay. One pressing issue was identifying enough nurses to stay on for an extra shift, so that all beds would be monitored. Staffing, whose desk was next to air traffic control, was at work on this problem.

Scott studied the board and worried over whether the hospital had adequate ICU space to receive comatose, intu-bated patients. He asked how many of the current ICU patients were well enough to be bumped out, if necessary, because they didn't really need ICU level care.

The nurse told him there were two "bumpables" in the cardiac ICU, two in the burn ICU (the "BI," she called it), and one in the medical ICU. She pointed at the patients' tags as she talked. The larger issue was that the floors were utter gridlock, owing to the fifty new admissions, so there was no place to put the bumpables.

Scott nodded, thanked the nurses, and promised to check back in a little later on. He walked upstairs, and Alice and Bob corralled him immediately. From Scott's point of view, the ED appeared to be functioning smoothly—impressively so in its level of coordination with physi-cians at the hyperbaric chamber. Alice and Bob wanted to discuss where the patients they were admitting would be going; every slot on the ED whiteboard just outside the radio room door was filled, and the hospital census Web site in the radio room showed three of the seven nearby hospitals in red, signifying an ED divert. The remaining hospitals plus Harborview were yellow, which meant that shipping patients elsewhere was out of the question. Every ED in the area was flooded with people affected by the windstorm, and every hospital was having trouble keeping track of all of the patients. Bob wondered aloud whether he might need to go up to the floors and encourage discharges that might create a few open beds, especially if patients with worse CO poisoning began arriving. "Let's hope it doesn't come to that," Scott said.

Around midnight, patients from the first dive group returned to the ED, and a second batch was sent over. An outside call rang through to the radio room, and Alice dashed to the door, tapped out the code, and reached for the phone. An emergency generator at a nearby hospital had gone down, she learned, and the hospital had two pending hip fractures requiring urgent fixation, plus a case of appendicitis, which was of course a surgical emergency. She glanced at the hospital census Web site, which was entirely red now, indicating that every ED and hospital in the city had reached their saturation level.

All closed equals all open, she thought. A number of months prior, the consortium of local hospitals that had put together Catch and Release had also agreed that all EDs and hospitals would reopen if half were closed. So Alice told the caller that she hoped their generator would get fixed soon, and to go ahead and send the patients when an ambulance could be found. She would help to get these patients to the OR, she said, and they would have to scare up the bed space and staffing somehow.

"All closed equals all open," Alice said out loud, as she hung up the phone. The private ambulance company American Medical Rescue (AMR) rang through on another line to say it was breaking with usual protocol and for the next few hours would transport patients to whichever hospital was nearest to the patient, even if the ED was packed, even if the hospital was private, even if the patient had no health insurance, even if the ED staff had yelled at the company's EMTs during the previous delivery.

At about 2 a.m., the ED social workers sent twenty-one patients to warm, lighted rooms at the First Hill Executive Suites, where they could stay until their own home electricity returned. Nurses and volunteers unfolded additional cots in the hospital cafeteria for the patients who continued to arrive, requiring hospitalization. And amazingly, the hospital doors remained open for business, Alice noted. There would be no Catch and Release, no ambulance divert tonight. *All closed equals all open. All closed equals all open.*

Alice left the hospital at 3 a.m. so she could get cleaned up, gather her things, and head to the airport with her husband. By that hour, most of the day shift attendings who had stayed past their shift had gone home, and the on-call residents came down from their work on the hospital floors to help care for the patients. Twice, as new waves of patients arrived, Bob felt as though the ED had just used its last sandbag. By sunrise, the Harborview ED had evaluated and treated fifty-nine people for carbon monoxide, and the stack of new charts began dwindling. Scott, who had stayed overnight monitoring operations in the hospital, went home to sleep. Copass dialed in and told Bob that the 140 patients at the neighborhood nursing home would be staying put, that the Fire Department had fixed the nursing home's broken emergency generator.

Later Bob would come to think of Copass's behind-the-scenes effort as one major piece in keeping the hospital operational. "A bolus of 140 patients would have brought us to our knees," he told me. In the meantime, Copass had been in touch with various members of the community, asking them to please spread the word about the dangers of indoor burning. Among his community contacts was the Orange Cab Company, an outfit that employed a number of Somali drivers; the taxi drivers were out and about on the roads, warning family members and friends that carbon monoxide could kill. Bob marveled how all of Copass's seemingly random and arcane knowledge had come together in a patchwork plan to organize and galvanize the community, to keep the medical system from suffering complete overload.

Their telephone conversation turned to the press conference that was scheduled for 11 a.m., which Bob would be hosting. Copass emphasized how important it was for the media to educate the community that carbon monoxide was a very real and deadly risk. Bob agreed, and he hung up feeling good about the morning. He drove home to see his wife and ate a bowl of cereal, happy for a few minutes with his usual routine. He slept forty minutes, arose, showered, and returned to the hospital, where he faced a zealous press who seemed to him to be most interested in why these people weren't getting into their cars and driving around to stay warm, like everybody else. Were these people stupid?

Bob stared at the reporters in disbelief and his brain tried to form a few diplomatic sentences. These are people who are poor, who don't have cars, who can't afford gas, he said. Some of the patients were non–English-speaking immigrants from warmer parts of the world, and they were accustomed to keeping cooking fires indoors, in houses that weren't sealed tightly, like American houses were. Others had run generators inside, not realizing they were poisoning themselves with carbon monoxide, which was odorless and colorless and generated no alarm. Bob emphasized that there were people in the community who were still at risk, that reporters could save lives by educating readers on the hazards of indoor burning. Interest in lifesaving seemed tepid. Bob took a few questions and then ended the conference.

He was scheduled to work the noon to 8 p.m. shift that day, and he thought he might as well get back to work.

To everyone's dismay, safety tips on carbon monoxide weren't prominently featured in the newspapers until the fourth day of the blackout.

Later, Bob was grateful that the volume of CO poisonings had petered out almost as quickly as they had begun; every hospital in Seattle had been besieged but began digging out some ten hours later. In the middle of the night it hadn't been quite so clear that the tide would recede so quickly, though. Some had opined that the poisonings might continue to roll in for several days, until electricity was restored in the city, and Bob wasn't confident that the hospital could have absorbed so many extra patients for so many additional days.

"We don't have the capacity we always had," he told me. "We're kind of like Wal-Mart, with our just-in-time inventory." He had been struck by how fragile the hospital had seemed as the disaster was unfolding, the all-night prospect that the next hit might carry them over the edge. He also wondered whether his sky-is-falling perspective reflected his own inexperience. "Maybe once you've been through a big disaster, you realize that you just make it through," he said. He hadn't known what to expect, hadn't known how long the staff could have kept working at that intensity before they became totally exhausted. Much of the efforts on behalf of the public's health could never have been captured in a detailed disaster plan or drilled into the staff. So many of the true heroes of the blackout were rank-and-file Harborview staff like Dana Williams in the hospital's interpreter services program, who posted flyers in grocery stores and housing projects that warned against indoor grills and generators; like Kim Lundgren, a Vietnamese language and cultural interpreter who covered local churches and temples; and like Fadumo Aden, a medical assistant in the pediatric clinic who covered many miles in the cities of Tukwila and SeaTac, educating refugees about the deadly gas.

Bob believed that the specific circumstances of the blackout had proven lucky for the hospital: many individuals had gladly stayed a few extra hours or for an additional shift, because they would otherwise be headed back to unheated, unpowered homes. He felt that the health care system might not always be so fortunate. There was mounting evidence that surge capacity, or the ability to respond to a mass casualty incident, was seriously overstretched everywhere. Public hospitals were at the center of most disaster relief efforts, because many were the primary trauma centers for their region, and disaster preparedness depended in part on open beds in these hospitals. Because of several hospital closures, many of the surviving public hospitals operated at full capacity on a routine basis, like Harborview, which could pose a real challenge if the hospital needed to absorb a sudden surge of patients. (Most hospitals had contingency plans to expand into spaces like the hospital cafeteria, or nearby churches and schools, in the event of a true disaster.)

In addition, there were concerning questions about the on-demand availability of medical workers. The widespread shortage of nurses, which affected public hospitals disproportionately, was one critical issue. There was the possibility that in a flu pandemic some workers would be deterred from reporting for duties because of the transmissible nature of the disease. And then there was the question of how long those who came to work could realistically stay on to help. After Hurricane Katrina, staff at one hospital had remained in-house for eight days, tending to the patients. When

FEMA finally arrived to offer medical backup, the agency found itself keeping dozens of children occupied while their parents cared for the patients, and watching forty-five dogs, fifteen cats, and two guinea pigs.

December's blackout in Seattle fell quickly from the head-lines, and afterward, in times of normalcy, there seemed to be less urgency to prepare the community for future disas-ters. The emergency response was widely felt to have been effective, and public leaders focused on how everybody had pulled together to help out. But as Bob and his colleagues pointed out, these carbon monoxide poisonings had been predated by a similar event, some years prior, albeit on a smaller scale. Strenuous attempts led by Neil Hampton, medical director for Virginia Mason's hyperbaric chamber, to warn about a coming large-scale carbon monoxide poi-soning had yielded very little in the way of preventive mea-sures to protect public health. It was as though the biggest question that remained after a disaster had to do with the community's capacity to learn from its experience, its will-ingness to transform itself.

Under Construction

Scott Barnhart kicked off the next staff meeting by thanking everyone for their efforts during the blackout. Dozens of patients with carbon monoxide poisoning had come through the ED in an eight-hour period, and the doors stayed open to everyone else. He smiled and said that the manpower in the ED had been a sight to behold. A little cheer went up in the crowd. I was sitting in back with Alice and some of the other junior faculty members. Alice sighed. She was wearing a cell phone and three pagers on her belt, which marked her as the emergency communications person of the day.

Fifty patients were discharged the morning after the poisonings, Scott reported, which represented about one-seventh of all positive hospital beds, probably a record day for discharges.

"We've been running at a very high occupancy ever since," he said. He put up the first of his slides on the hospital's financials. Harborview would clear $3 million on $900 million in clinical charges in 2006, enough to keep the lights turned on and medical supplies arriving on schedule, but the coming year faced an $18 million budget shortfall. This was very concerning, Scott said, and the administration had put together several initiatives to help close the gap. He asked everyone to watch for these and to plan on participating. Many of the organization's obvious inefficiencies had been addressed in prior process improvement efforts, and the hospital would have to work increasingly harder for smaller gains in efficiency.

A graph showing growth in use of the electronic medical record came up on the screen. Scott thanked everybody who had switched to the new system, which was helping with patient safety and with hospital communications, and had accelerated billings and collections significantly.

The major agenda issue that day was a report on the two new towers being erected north and east of the original 1931 hospital building. Scott introduced Johnese Spisso, the hospital's COO, whom I glimpsed occasionally in the elevators scrolling through email on her handheld PDA. She was wearing a purple suit and a colorful neck scarf, and she reported that the new inpatient building, which would add fifty new ICU beds, was on track to open in two years. The massive steel frame was already in place, as was the skeleton for a skybridge connecting the old and new buildings. In just a few weeks, hundreds of miles of electrical wire and PVC pipe had been laid down by a small army of workers who arrived at dawn wearing white hard hats and carrying their lunches in plastic coolers.

Across the street from the new inpatient facility would be a new outpatient building, which had mushroomed in size from five stories to fourteen, with nearly half a million square feet of clinic and office space in the plan. Financing had finally been secured, Spisso reported, after Harborview had guaranteed $13 million per year to service the debt, and construction was underway. An architect's rendition of the future campus flashed on the screen; in the drawings,

Harborview looked like a small mountain range made from cement and glass.

"Whatever it takes to block out the other hospitals," a faculty member joked.

Spisso smiled broadly as she listed off keystone franchises for the new facilities, including the HIV, Sleep, Rehabilitation, Neuroscience, and Spine centers, plus the medical examiner's office and the new global health department, all programs that represented the exciting, glamorous future of the hospital. She described the Spine Center, which was already functional, as an elite service station where patients visited neurosurgeons, orthopedists, neurologists, medical consultants, and pain specialists all in one stop. After receiving their complicated back surgeries, patients could return for physical and occupational therapy and continuing rehabilitation. The center brought in people from all over the world, she said, and Harborview was hard at work on plans for centers that served those with other surgically remediable diseases, like broken hips.

A surgeon inquired politely about parking.

A five-story garage would open a full year ahead of the buildings, providing six hundred new spaces, she answered, and then added, "Parking helps us pay the rent." The monthly fee had increased to $200 for the main lot.

I saw that Scott was grinning. He had recently given up his beloved "global warmer," as he called his old Suburban, and was jetting about the city by public transportation.

As I walked back to the hospital, I wondered how long it would be after the new inpatient building opened that the fifty extra beds would prove inadequate and Harborview would have to retrofit existing space or develop additional property. Would it be a month? A year? Two years? Fifty beds did not sound like very much additional capacity, given that the current census often ran in the negative double digits and in the previous months had hit thirty to forty negative beds. Plus, the new beds weren't really for the poor and indigent patients who were "managed" at the front door when the hospital was full. They were primarily critical care and surgical beds, to capture the sorts of cases that could generate significant revenue for the hospital.

I was very much aware of the tension between the hospital's clinical mission of serving patients regardless of ability to pay and its operating mandate of running a positive margin—its need to make a slim profit, in other words. This tension derived partly from the fact that Harborview was not a classically public institution, nor was it really a business enterprise that assumed big financial risks to bring new services to the market. However, I was coming to believe that Harborview's particular mixture of charity and commerce made more sense than either of the more traditional organizational models. Thanks to the blend of margin and mission, the hospital operated very efficiently and provided high quality health care to all comers, including many of the region's most vulnerable individuals.

I also recognized that durable health care for vulnerable populations was possible only as long as Harborview remained open. There had been six hospitals serving Seattle's indigent in the late 1970s, and currently there was only Harborview, which had no special immunity against closure or reduction in services. Even Providence Hospital, the city's original poor hospital, had been sold and transformed into a temple for highly profitable cardiac and neurosurgical procedures. One of the reasons that Harborview had remained open was because it had learned to get by without significant public assistance, which allowed the hospital to remain fully functional in years when funding was scarce. The extent of public support that Harborview received was a $7 million annual supplement from the state legislature to fund physician training, plus higher trauma reimbursements for Medicaid patients. In addition, the county government episodically helped to raise funds for new construction or renovation of existing buildings. But these measures paled in comparison with the $140 million in yearly infusions that similar institutions like San Francisco General Hospital received from the government. And even with these massive appropriations, some public hospitals were still hemorrhaging tens if not hundreds of millions of dollars every year.

It was starting to seem that Harborview was operationally sound because it behaved like a business. The hospital administration worked continuously to increase the efficiency and quality of medical care delivered: there were ongoing customer service initiatives, a heroic campaign to transform the hospital's information technologies, and intensive efforts to increase bed availability through the newly hired discharge nurse, whose entire role was to get patients out the door so that those waiting in the ED could get a bed. At times it seemed that the administration was trying to squeeze money from stone, as with the new parking garage, which would open a year ahead of the buildings they would serve, and with the in-services for clinicians on "optimizing" documentation in the medical chart, to ensure that all clinical activities were being "captured." And then there was the issue of labor costs, which were far and away Harborview's greatest expense. Physicians and nurses and executives earned a fraction of the going rate in the private sector, as little as one-third to one-half what could be made elsewhere. And yet the job vacancy rate and turnover were the lowest in the metropolitan area.

Despite the administration's strenuous efforts, though, the hospital's financials no longer looked as bulletproof as they once had. Charity care was growing at $10 to $40 million per year, which had forced the administration to seek more generous revenue streams, and this quest had ultimately placed the hospital at the mercy of the health care market. Health care is a vast market in the United States, accounting for some $2 trillion worth of business, or 16 percent of the total U.S. gross domestic product.

Much of health care purchasing is controlled by the federal Medicare and Medicaid programs, which bought $655 billion worth of health care goods and services in 2005, or 30 percent of the total market, which enabled the government to essentially set prices for most health care services. Through a political process controlled by specialist physicians, Medicare determined that the health care services of greatest value were the risky, complex surgical procedures and critical care services. Strangely, the market (Medicare) did not address the issue of whether health care actually made patients healthier. Nor did the market address the issue of the tens of millions of individuals without health insurance, even though it absorbed all of the costs of caring for these people when they became ill.

In any case, Harborview's long-range plan catered to what the market valued. The hospital was being transformed into a center "offering leading edge programs in trauma, burn, neurosciences, AIDS/STD, critical care, and other specialized tertiary care services to patients from all walks of life," and an overhaul of the hospital's product line and brand image had begun in earnest. The first of the specialty surgical centers had moved into its own beautiful, brand-new facility, away from the original hospital building. State-of-the-art operating facilities were under construction, and patient services had been streamlined so that patients could move in a smooth arc from the intake clinics to the operating rooms, into the hospital, and then to rehabilitation.

An image makeover was equally crucial to the hospital's clinical transformation, since a facility that served jail patients and drug addicts and drunks was not necessarily the sort of place that respectable, middle-class citizens might seek out voluntarily. In came Pamela Steele, a former vice president at a local television station and a public relations expert who had also worked for the Peace Corps in Sudan. Steele was charged with telling the public a new story about the hospital, and I visited her one afternoon to learn about her ideas. An energetic woman with short stylish hair and sharp blue eyes, Steele said to me, "We can be your hospital of choice in addition to being the hospital of necessity. What we're trying to communicate is that patients choose us because of the expertise our physicians offer. A lot of people don't realize that our entire medical staff is University of Washington faculty."

To illustrate her point, she reached into a file cabinet and handed me a recent annual report that her office had produced, an elegant booklet printed on beautiful, heavy paper. The first vignette described a real estate developer from Washington D.C. who flew cross-country to visit with his trusted brain surgeon at Harborview. The patient enjoyed restoring old military vehicles and building furniture from scratch, and the report stressed that he continued to do so thanks to multiple successful operations to remove a rare form of brain tumor, which regenerated itself every few years. His neurosurgeon at the county hospital was the world-renown Laligam Sekhar, revered for his operative innovation and his skillful hands. Half of Sekhar's elective cases come from out of the state, and a number from out of the country, Steele said. The fact was that patients were choosing Harborview for the physician expertise.

Steele told me that five-star Army general and former Joint Chief of Staffs General John Shalikashvili had selected Harborview's inpatient rehabilitation program after suffering a severe hemorrhagic stroke several years earlier. She noted that the *U.S. News & World Report* had for a number of years running ranked the joint Harborview/ university hospital rehabilitation program as the best in the entire country. This was the sort of information that the health consumer needed to know in order to make informed decisions about their medical care, she suggested. The story of the new Harborview was a story about smart customers coming for edgy treatment strategies, world-class surgeons, and empathetic staff.

It was a far cry from Pat Fleet's drunk who looked up from a gutter to the hospital shining on the hill.

In any case, public and private institutions around the country had taken note of Harborview's particular blend of service and business. The proof lay with executives like Johnese Spisso. She had worked as a trauma nurse and made her way up to the number two position at the hospital. She was routinely recruited for CEO jobs in health care systems around the country and had declined the top job at another major Seattle hospital a few years before. That that institution had offered to triple her salary was a testament to her individual worth on the open market and was also a statement about the appeal of the management ideas that the administration have developed at Harborview, where desperation was the mother of invention.

Providing ongoing access to medical care was an impressive achivement, one that very few hospitals or health systems in our country managed to offer with the same depth and breadth as Harborview. But access did not necessarily translate into health. Despite the hospital's success at keeping the doors open, it seemed that many patients were as exposed and vulnerable to severe illness as ever before, and that the small gains we achieved through hospital care were often temporary.

With my homeless patients in particular, it was clear that securing housing, warm clothing, and meals was a full-time concern, and that adherence to a medical plan was secondary. One reason I believed that patients looked so good after two or three days in the hospital was that they hadn't had to worry about finding shelter and nourishment, because they could get sleep without worrying about having their things stolen, because they could readily get a hot shower, as much as their improved state could be attributed to anything that we had done. If anything, it was the sympathetic and attentive care that the nurses provided that explained why patients improved rapidly, since many had no family or good friends to help them through their illness. Recognizing this, it was impossible not to believe that larger social inequalities played a very significant role in poor health.

As Scott Barnhart said to me, "The primary predictor of health status is educational outcomes, not clinical care." Health care, at least of the high-intensity, high-technology sort that we provided, did very little to help patients overcome the larger structural inequalities that existed in society, like the lack of affordable housing or the cost of obtaining adequate nutrition.

Many clinicians who worked with underserved patients remarked to me over the years that they entered medicine in hopes of making a difference in people's lives. As they gained practice experience, though, these clinicians came to recognize that using insulin appropriately was practically beside the point when you weren't sure whether you were going to be able to eat. Were doctors making a real difference for these people? It was hard to know. So much energy had been spent in fighting to preserve access to medical care that there wasn't much left over to think cohesively about what really helped people maintain health, and whether the underserved might in fact benefit from different or additional health services. And perhaps because this population was viewed as both transient and unprofitable, there had been very little innovation specifically addressing the care of these individuals. Basically, we waited until these patients came to the ED before thinking about how to help.

So what could be done? Well, plenty, but it might not involve unconditional access to things like MRIs and the very newest medications. For one thing, structural inequalities could be addressed directly, as Scott Barnhart had done when he stepped off the academic fast track fifteen years ago to serve on the Seattle school board. He and his wife had considered placing their children in private schools, but they recognized that an exodus of families like theirs from the public school system would weaken the schools, and that meant greater inequalities in education, which reinforced the gap between rich and poor in ways that were very durable.

It was better to work within public institutions to effect change and seek equality, he believed; this was society's best shot at eliminating, or at least reducing, poverty. He told me that he was most proud during his tenure on the school board when the district implemented a weighted formula that disproportionately allocated funds to students who needed them the most. The policy challenged conventional wisdom in the education world but was ultimately struck down by the U.S. Supreme Court in 2007.

Programs that pushed the envelope were exactly what was needed to address the needs of the medically underserved, but there had been little innovation in the care of this population, in spite of the reasoning that healthy patients generally consumed less health care and might therefore be less expensive for society. Of course, there were costs and risks in innovation, and when you already stood to lose money, the margin for error was narrow and the risks seemed even higher. There was the particular risk that any investment in disease prevention or ongoing chronic care of illness might be squandered if a patient moved to another hospital system, which happened not infrequently with this group of people. (This is one argument for universal, single-payer health care, which would create a closed system and make one entity responsible for improving health.) But the serious challenge of creating something novel, of creating a genuine innovation for the underserved didn't become clear to me until something truly revolutionary presented itself.

Bunks for Drunks

Thanks to an experimental wet house in the downtown area, Seattle's most expensive homeless alcoholics like Elaine Cook had a place to call home—studios of their own furnished with a twin bed, stovetop, and a three-quarter bath, plus a personal refrigerator where they could chill beer if they wished. The house did not require Elaine to partake in its social services, which included case management, medical assistance, and two chemical dependency counselors on site at all times. All Elaine had to do in order to retain her spot was hand over 30 percent of her monthly check, as rent, and not beat anybody up, which she was probably not going to do. If she followed the two house rules, she was welcome to stay until she died.

While trying to learn more about the wet house, I met Bill Hobson, executive director of the Downtown Emergency Service Center, the umbrella housing organization that sponsored the project. At Harborview we had noticed that some patients weren't in the ED or the hospital as often as before, I said, and we believed it had to do with his novel project. I mentioned that I was writing a book and was curious what the place was like.

Hobson said, "You wouldn't believe how many calls I get about that place. I could have a reporter there every day of the year. Thankfully, I don't get attacked nearly as often as I used to." He had just finished entertaining someone from *The New York Times*. He paused and then said, "When do you want to come by? I'll give you the tour myself."

Conventional wisdom says that homelessness is a lifestyle choice, that the homeless aren't interested in the rules and structure of conventional social life. Conventional wisdom says that homeless people who want housing should work for their shelter by remaining sober or complying with mental illness treatment, by developing the "skills" needed to remain housed, and eventually, by working toward employment. The problem with these ideas, Hobson told me, is the forty-five-year-old man who has been drinking for fifteen years and has been through alcohol treatment six times or more. Longitudinal public health data suggests that in all likelihood, this person will die before he becomes sober.

"What are we going to do with a guy like this?" Hobson asked. I was sitting with him and Alice Brownstein at a table in the dining room of the facility, under humming fluorescent lights. He was a bespectacled man with a white beard who wore sneakers, jeans, and a Seahawks sweatshirt. One of the residents wandered into the dining area and helped himself to a slice of the chocolate sheet cake on the kitchen counter. Hobson said, "Conventional treatment doesn't work for this sort of person. So what does?"

He answered his own question: "We know that doing nothing doesn't work." There was "startling" mortality in this population, and before these individuals died, they made frequent visits to county mental health, detox, jail, and of course to the Harborview ED. The costs were frequently enormous, suggesting that a passive approach to this particular subpopulation was ineffective.

The hypothesis underpinning the wet house was that treatment of mental illness and substance abuse might be more effective when a homeless person's need for stable housing was met first, because housing could then precipitate other life changes. The model had been pilot-tested in several cities, including New York City and San Francisco, and early results had shown that in certain populations, stable housing created a significant drop-off in the consumption of public services and also reduced the number of costly ED visits. Two co-investigators at Seattle's University of Washington had been granted funds from the Robert Wood Johnson Foundation to study the housing project over a three-year period.

Despite promising results in other cities, even the concept attracted plenty of critics. Before construction could begin, the Benaroya family, which owned office towers down the street (and for whom Seattle's Symphony Hall was named), filed suit with Hobson's organization over a zoning issue. The DESC won, and then won again on appeal—"We beat his brains out," Hobson claimed—but the suit took years to fight, and it was enough to derail the building's financing. Hobson suspected that was the family's original intent anyway.

Five years after the original ground-breaking had been scheduled, the building permits and financing were restored, and construction on the four-story tower finally began. But the opposition only grew louder. *The Seattle Times* rejected the idea of using public money for apartments where residents were allowed to drink; this was just common sense, the newspaper argued. KOMO TV's Ken Schram lampooned the facility as a booze palace, where residents were allowed to party with their buddies and run wild. The belief seemed to be that the only way to deal with the poor was with carrots and sticks. Public tolerance for innovation was low, when it came to "those people."

Construction finished in December 2005, and the selection of residents proceeded from a list of the two hundred people who consumed the most county resources.

"We started with the most expensive individual and made our way down the list," Hobson said. The first three were dead, the fourth couldn't be found, the fifth was located and invited to live there. "We had seventy-five beds, and we only had to ask seventy-nine people in order to fill the building." The first residents moved in at Christmas 2005, and the building was full three months later. Hobson added, "I never put much stock in that whole hobo consciousness. I think it's a bunch of bullshit. If you offer these guys a place to live, they will take it." One prospective resident even said to him, "I've been hearing about this for a year. It's about time."

I asked why residents weren't compelled to participate in the services that were available. He said, "This was a deliberate strategy. We thought it was far better to romance them, to get them to choose to engage with us, than it was to coerce." A year into the project, the initial results were promising: the majority were drinking less than when they were on the streets, eight residents became abstinent, and several moved into sober housing, where the support for abstinence was very strong.

Success had not come without speed bumps, however. In its first year of operation, the staff placed dozens of calls to 911. "We expected a medically fragile population, but we just had no idea," Hobson said. In hindsight, the degree of illness probably shouldn't have been so surprising, since the county's most expensive individuals were, by definition, in the ED routinely. As staff became more accustomed to the residents' conditions, though, the emergency calls dropped off, and attendings in the Harborview ED were reporting fewer visits from certain patients. Medication compliance among residents was around 80 percent, up from 20 percent, which suggested that mental illness was under better control in that group. The gains were coming at a cost of about $15,000 per resident per year, about the cost of two or three ED visits.

The Seattle Times later carried a conciliatory editorial written by a city attorney, who described a number of the residents of the wet house as chronic offenders who had appeared regularly in the courts and in jail. He wrote, "Since the apartments opened, we hardly see them at all."

Hobson, Alice, and I stood and embarked on a lap of the ground floor, passing though the television room, which looked like a Saturday morning in a college dorm room: five or six residents were watching a basketball game and one was reading the newspaper. We glimpsed the laundry facilities, intended for use by residents but generally manned by staff, Hobson told us, because most residents had a hard time completing all of the steps needed to get their clothes washed. It was amazing how debilitating long-term alcohol use was, he observed. The facility, which had then been open for a year and a half, still had a little bit of new building smell. The smoking porch out back was empty.

Hobson led us past the ground-floor sleeping areas and pointed out where the more notorious characters slept; Alice recognized many of the names, having seen them at some point in the ED. We got in the elevator with one of the residents, a Native American man who bounced on his toes while he waited. Hobson made small talk. A computer-generated sign that was taped to the elevator wall said, "Peaceful and calm . . . Peaceful and calm . . . Peaceful and calm." We exited on the top floor and Hobson led us into an unoccupied efficiency studio, pointing out the unit's safety features, including a timer that activated and automatically turned off the stove, and the central drain on the bathroom floors, in case a resident forgot and left the water running. He pointed to the refrigerator to show us where the residents could store beer, if they desired, and when he opened the door, I almost expected to see a six-pack, having heard so much about the house's alcohol policy. The refrigerator was empty.

Hobson shut the door and said, "What does an alcoholic who lives on the streets do all day? He gets up and starts thinking about what he's going to drink. Maybe it depends on how much money he's got. So he goes to the store and gets himself a fifth, if he has the funds, or a bottle of cheap wine or malt liquor, and then he drinks it immediately. All of it. That's because he could bump into his buddies, who will want to share, or a cop will ask him to pour it out. So he gets it down as fast as he can, and that holds him for a while. When the alcohol wears off he's got to start the cycle over again. The thing about living here is that when you buy your fifth, you don't have to finish it first thing in the morning. You can leave it in your unit and go do something else. It's a lot easier on the body that way."

We studied the view from the window, and Hobson pointed in the direction of a neighborhood convenience mart where residents sometimes purchased their alcohol. His organization had worked to have certain favored beverages withdrawn from local stores, he said, to keep the worst stuff away. Alice and I nodded as we exited the studio and headed back down to the main reception area, where flyers advertised guitar lessons, library outings, baseball games.

Hobson said, "We're trying to help them remember the life they had at one time." He even considered building a sweat lodge in the basement, since one-third of the residents were Native American, and "sweating" was believed to be a healing, purifying cultural practice that he thought could help residents fight their alcoholism and also recognize their heritage. But he shook his head and said, "Not going to happen. I can just picture the headline: 'Luxury Hotel for Drunks.'"

We walked into view of the dining hall, and Elaine Cook was sitting at one of the tables, tucking into a piece of chocolate cake. She looked up at us and asked for something. Hobson moved toward her, caught what Elaine was saying, then walked to the kitchen island and tore off a paper towel.

"Thank you, darling," Elaine said. Alice was being very quiet, and I saw that she was watching Elaine's arthritic hands negotiate the paper towel, watching her wipe frosting slowly from each of her fingers.

Finally she asked, "How do you like the cake, Elaine?"

"Delicious," she answered, looking up at Alice with confusion. *She doesn't remember Alice*, I realized.

Alice looked at her with an expression of wonder. She said, "It's really good to see you, Elaine. You look wonderful."

"Thank you, ma'am."

"You have a good day."

"You have a good day, ma'am." Elaine returned her attention to the cake, and we walked back into the front lobby, where Hobson said, "The woman is a testament to the resilience of the human body."

He faced Alice and said, "Michael Copass is my hero."

"Copass is my hero," Alice said, smiling.

We thanked Hobson for the time he'd taken, for his efforts to keep some of the most vulnerable people housed, and shook hands all around. Hobson said, "We're trying to meet them where they're at."

"We'll all be interested in the data," I said.

"So will I," Hobson replied.

Outside, it was cold and windy. For a moment, Alice and I stood talking over the roof of her car. They could probably still see us on the closed-circuit television monitor behind the front desk.

"Elaine doesn't look too bad."

"She looks so old." Alice smiled sadly. "God, I forgot how slowly she moves." We got in the car, and she told me about someone else who had been a frequent flyer in the ED, an older man who had moved into the wet house, got himself cleaned up, and finally stopped drinking. He'd returned to the ED at one point to say hello to everybody, and a few weeks later had died in his bed during the night. He'd suffered from advanced liver failure. Alice put her sunglasses on, started the car, and said, "I don't know. He was going to die anyway. He probably lived a few extra months because he had a roof over his head. And he got to die with dignity."

For Sale

The hospital was still recuperating from the carbon monoxide poisonings for many weeks afterward. Toward the end of January, the census again hit fifty negative beds. The hospital had been flirting with medic divert for weeks, and the ED was closed to ambulances on a routine basis. A young Vietnamese man woke from a weeks-long coma, the only one of five household members to survive an indoor poisoning, and his beautiful wife arrived from Asia. The timing seemed fortuitous. And then, devastatingly, he died two days later.

On the wards, the homeless and debilitated eighty-one-year-old Howard Short was still on my service. He was finally scheduled to appear in court that morning, but when his wheelchair arrived, he refused to go. He declared that he wasn't going to miss lunch, and he brushed off his nurse's promises to keep his food warm. The judge agreed that Short was incapable of making decisions and appointed a guardian, who met with him not long afterward. The guardian opined that Short should go to a nursing home, even though he very understandably preferred home, and Barb had a bed reserved for Short within the hour. She sent me a text page saying that he was set for discharge that afternoon.

I called Barb back to tell her I'd finish the paperwork as soon as I saw Geoff Morgan, the VIP who'd secured one of the private rooms on Three, and who was waiting to see me. Morgan was a sixty-five-year-old who had been diagnosed with leukemia a few years back, on routine blood tests. He'd been hospitalized several times since, for simple things like a blood transfusion or to get a diagnostic test done, and he'd get whisked back home by his wife, Nanette, who never missed a beat. This year his disease had transformed from a smoldering annoyance into something vaguely more sinister, and now his blood was clogged with cancer cells. Morgan and his wife had opted for aggressive chemotherapy, which his oncologist had described as sometimes curative, if patients proceeded to bone marrow transplantation.

That was an "if." The first chemotherapy cocktail hadn't worked—the tumor had continued growing unchecked—so they'd opted for an even more toxic regimen, and it wasn't clear that one was working either. Plus, chemo had made Morgan susceptible to unusual infections, because the drugs suppressed his immune system, and once he'd gotten so sick that it kept him from continuing chemotherapy, at least for a while. This time he was again being admitted with a high fever.

When I came into the room, Morgan said, "Hi, you. It's your lucky day." He was trying to be cheerful, but he sounded bleak. He was curled up in a pair of flannel pajamas from home.

I asked Nanette how she was doing. She sighed and said, "We were managing fine. But this, it's too much." In addition to the high fever, he'd been retching bile for days, which was the pattern following the new regimen.

"So, what's the bad news, slugger?" Morgan asked.

"We're going to do some tests," I said.

"Tests," he said. "I can't seem to pass them lately."

"We'll be giving strong antibiotics to cover a lot of different bugs until we figure out what this is."

"So you'll wait to find out what it is before shooting me." He chuckled weakly. I knew he was trying to lighten the mood, but the remark came off a bit oddly. Nanette was frowning.

I said, "It's possible we won't find anything. Sometimes it's just how bodies respond to these drugs."

"Which tests will you be ordering?" Nanette asked. She was holding a pad of yellow legal paper and was poised to write.

"We'll start with cultures plus a chest X-ray."

"Blood cultures, urine cultures, stool cultures?" Nanette asked.

I nodded.

"And CT scans? To see if the lymph nodes have shrunk? And whether that pneumonia came back."

"Right," I said. "My preference is to start with the X-ray and cultures. I think we'll gain some information there. It would be good to give the chemotherapy some time to work before another scan." With the Morgans, I made my suggestions, but the treatment plan was never finalized before Nanette gave the OK.

She tapped her pen against her lips and said, "Can you explain that?"

I sighed and began trying to answer the question. Fifteen minutes later, Morgan was sound asleep and Nanette seemed more or less satisfied.

She gave me a wide, glossy smile and said, "Thank you for your excellent care."

Actually, I liked Morgan and his wife, and I imagined I might act just the same in her shoes. I especially liked Morgan's sense of humor, even if it came out awkwardly sometimes. But in general I had mixed feelings about how the hospital treated VIPs. VIPs got private rooms just so they could get some rest. VIPs could refuse medications and therapies without being lectured on how the hospital needed beds for those patients who wanted treatment. I did not think that VIPs who asserted their status got better medical care, and this was not only because we genuinely tried to give the same excellent care to all patients. When a patient or a patient's family got bossy, it threw everyone off course, and sometimes we became too cautious or too aggressive for what the situation required. I wondered whether the plan would have been bone-shaking chemotherapy followed by transplant if Morgan weren't a VIP. I didn't think there was any way he could survive such an intensive procedure, which was a near-death experience for even the healthiest people. Had he been steered toward less aggressive therapy, maybe he'd experience less suffering and have more quality time to spend with Nanette. These were likely to be his last months after all.

I went into one of the ward workrooms with a few charts, paged the oncology fellow, and thought again about whether Morgan should have more CT scans. The scans would show whether there was an abscess hidden somewhere, although it was more likely to show nothing of consequence and only expose him to more radiation. Still, getting the test would be the path of least resistance in dealing with the Morgans. The fellow rang back.

"You know, I'm not sure how much time they think he has," I said.

"No, I know," he replied. He said that the attending oncologist wanted to press onward with chemotherapy, so we agreed to have a conference with the family in a day or so, when Morgan was hopefully feeling a little bit better. I thanked the fellow and turned to Howard Short's discharge paperwork. A moment later I picked up Morgan's chart again and wrote orders for his cultures, which I had just about forgotten.

A resident wandering through the workroom stopped me to tell me that she'd recently seen Hope Sheridan, the woman for whom we'd engineered the failed abuser-escape strategy. The resident said that Hope had gained some weight and looked good. Her cancer was in remission, and she had finally left her boyfriend, who was in jail for assaulting someone else. We both pulled up our white coats, crossed our arms, and shivered. Hope was living with her daughter and taking care of her grandkids so that her daughter could go back to work. I thanked the resident for the good news, then I turned to the chart of a fifty-year-old man named Bert Burphy, a salesman who had tumbled from his roof a month earlier, while cleaning his gutters, and shattered his right leg.

Burphy had been in the hospital for thirty-one days and had thus far undergone three surgeries and cheated death twice. He had survived what the radiologists called "one mother of a blood clot," which developed as a result of a rare clotting disorder, and which they then carefully dug out of his pulmonary arteries. Despite the fanciest of blood thinners after this initial episode, though, a new blood clot developed, causing significant swelling in both of his legs, and it extended to within inches of his heart. The radiologists had placed a filter just beyond the clot, at my urging, to prevent further migration. A few hours later, the pulse in his left foot disappeared and his leg began to die. The residents on the scene contacted the vascular surgery service about the emergent situation, and I left my dinner and drove back to the hospital, where Burphy reminded me that he had recently become engaged.

"You get me out of this hospital alive, and I will give up every bad habit and lose fifteen pounds," he said. His face expressed sheer terror. He said that the pain in his leg was excruciating, and he pleaded, "Please, do not let me die."

The vascular surgery attending was at the bedside moments later; he wore scrubs and carried a compact athletic bag. Soon he and his team were breaking up the clot in Burphy's legs, and by morning it looked again like Burphy had dodged a bullet. When I came by on my rounds, he told me that the leg pain had subsided immediately, that once more he had been saved by the surgeons. He wiped his brow, asked for ice chips, and wondered if I would be able to thank everyone for him.

In any case, the task of the day was to get him upright for the first time in weeks, and I wrote orders for both physical and occupational therapy visits. Burphy had played league hockey prior to his accident, and he had already started doing pull-ups from a bar that hung over his bed, but it would be a production even getting him to stand, since he had been bed-bound for a month and was subsequently very weak. In addition, he had a heavy metal contraption around his right leg, which stabilized his fracture externally, and which he referred to as his metal prison. The surgeons had asked him not to put any weight on the right foot until X-rays showed the bone starting to heal. I wrote for the blood-thinning medication, for a laboratory test to be drawn in the morning, and then liberalized his pain medications for use with activity.

As I was flagging all of the new orders and carrying the charts back to the nursing station carrel, where the ward clerk would pick them up, my pager rang. It was Geoff Morgan's nurse, calling to ask about the plan for the day. I thanked her for checking in and said I had written for cultures and increased his pain medications.

"Did you order that CT?"

"No CT. Not going to change the plan," I said and thanked her again for calling. With the Morgans, it was better that everybody was on the same page.

I peeked into Morgan's room again in the afternoon. He was snoring softly; this was the first he'd slept in days, Nanette told me. She was entertaining several luminaries in suits who had come by to wish them well. I saluted them and went off to find Burphy, who was sitting up reading the book *Succeeding in Your Own Business*, which his fiancée had given him for Christmas. His physical therapist had just been in, he said, and he'd finally stood up.

"Yup, I lasted about thirty seconds," he said. "If that. Head felt like it weighed 200 pounds." He had gotten sweaty and dizzy and needed a person to support him on each arm. But his rehabilitation was finally underway, and he looked energized. He was antsy to get mobile again, to get back to the rink, back to work, and above all, back to his fiancée. He was ready to launch out of the hospital, he said. I nodded my agreement and asked about the book he was reading.

He told me I could find his Web site via Google, if I wanted to check out his business selling plant-based supplements.

Later I found his Web site and clicked through photos of him on the rink, in his hockey gear, then clicked off his page and returned to the chart notes I had been putting off. *Thirty days in the hospital, and we turn Burphy inside and out*, I thought. *How come we never knew that about him?*

Geoff Morgan slept for most of the following three days and Nanette escaped the hospital to run errands she'd delayed for months. Morgan's initial cultures came back negative, so he eventually got the CT scans that Nanette had been pressing for. These showed no hidden infection, and no change in his lymph nodes. That afternoon Nanette, Morgan, and I convened with the attending oncologist to discuss the lack of progress. He suggested Morgan switch to a third regimen, an experimental protocol that might give them a little bit more time. Morgan looked pale and puffy from all of the fluids we had infused and he seemed exhausted, a different person than the cheery and funny guy he usually was.

"I got to tell you that I don't think I can do any more chemo," Morgan said.

The oncologist affected a concerned look. He moved forward, so he was sitting on the edge of his chair, and asked if Morgan was sure.

Nanette said, "Honey, do you know what you're saying?"

"Yes, I know what I'm saying," Morgan said crossly.

After a long pause he said, "I'm just so tired."

Later, when he was asleep again, I stood outside Morgan's door with Nanette, who was sobbing. She wasn't ready for him to go, she said. They had been best of friends for twenty years and had just gotten married. She couldn't imagine life without him. She wished he would just try one more course of chemo, because you never knew what might work.

She blew her nose and said, "I realize this is not about me. I know that he doesn't want any more chemo. But can't

I just have a couple more good months with him?" Within a moment she had collected herself, thanked me for listening, and announced that she had to get herself cleaned up. More luminaries were on the way.

By the end of the week, Bert Burphy had taken several steps with crutches, but he wasn't interested in talking about his breathing or his leg pain, because the first of his medical bills had just arrived in the mail. Today Burphy could only talk about how he had been charged $4,800 to visit the ED close to his home, after he'd fallen off his roof. That figure didn't include any medical care that he'd received at that first hospital, or the physician fees and the ambulance ride to Harborview, which would cost many thousands of dollars more. The bills didn't include his three surgeries, two ICU stays, two clot-busting procedures, a filter, weeks of rare and expensive blood thinners, physical therapy, pain medications, intravenous lines, or specialist fees. It didn't include the cost of his rehabilitation, which was still to come, or the reoperation planned for three months out, when his leg would be released from its metal prison. How would an uninsured salesman who worked for a modest middle-class income pay for his injury, even if he healed fully and returned to his former life?

I would send Barb in to talk with him, I said, and come back later in the day, since my pager had just rung three times. I hustled into a workroom to return the pages, which netted me another patient from the surgery service, a fellow in his forties who had been hit by a car while crossing the street in downtown Seattle, after enjoying three or four beers at happy hour. He had multiple fractures and was coming to the medicine service because of a post-fracture blood clot similar to Burphy's. On my way down to meet him, I dropped by Barb's office to ask about Burphy's financial status. She flipped through her binder and said that Burphy's Medicaid application had been submitted a couple of weeks ago and once he was approved, all of his costs would be covered as long as his disability lasted longer than ninety days.

"No problem. Ninety days is not going to be a problem for this person," I said. "Would you mind stopping by to talk with him and make sure he understands? He's real anxious about the money situation."

I zipped downstairs to see the man who'd been hit by a car, a commercial diver who was muscular and mustachioed and was watching tennis on ESPN. I asked how fast the car had been going when he was hit, he said, "You know, I wasn't really thinking about that as I was flying up onto the hood of the car."

"Sorry, you've probably been asked that question two dozen times."

"I wake up at four o'clock every morning with a dream that I'm about to be hit by a car. Do you think I can go home tomorrow?" He had good health insurance, he added, and in the meantime he wanted a private room.

I told him he would be clear from my standpoint as soon as we figured out the right dose of blood thinner. It was likely to be just a day or two more, but I didn't say this, since funding for the medication depended on just how good his insurance was.

He did not get a private room.

In the afternoon, my pager rang with a text message from a colleague that read, "KJ is back on Three—check out his HUGE family." KJ was the much beloved Kermit Jackson, jazz horn genius and temperamental Fleet patient.

I made my way to Three and swung past Kermit's room, which was packed with people wearing stylish dresses and felt hats. He was in a private room, and I thought immediately about how he had once come into the ED, gone into cardiac arrest, received an electrical shock to his chest, and came roaring back to life. He'd since had his right leg amputated and was diagnosed with liver cancer, which had caused severe bleeding in his abdomen the previous month. He hadn't been awake enough to recognize me during that hospitalization.

Before entering the room, I decided to search for Fleet to learn what was happening. Kermit was lucid again, Fleet told me, a little too lucid. He worried that Kermit was about to flip into mania.

"I mean, why is he in a private room? I didn't know he had so much family. Is he dying?" I asked.

Fleet said that Kermit was still getting dialysis, but that a kidney transplant was no longer in the works.

Later a colleague suggested that Fleet might be having a hard time, and I thought this seemed understandable, given how much he had been through with Kermit. Eventually I found out that Kermit was on comfort care and would be going to a nursing home when a bed opened.

When I came back later, Kermit grinned and said, "Hey, girl!" He had been receiving a steady stream of musicians all afternoon, and Grover Washington was playing on the computer jukebox in his room. We visited for a while, and as we talked about the illnesses he had suffered from for many years he said, "I've just had some real bad luck." Then he grinned again and asked if I could go to Chinatown and get him some red ginger and sour balls. I had no idea what he was talking about, but I said I would get him whatever he wanted. Fleet told me later that he'd forbidden Kermit from eating red ginger and sour balls years ago, when the salt load made him retain more fluid than could be removed with dialysis.

"Under the circumstances, though, we should probably let him eat what he wants."

"Great," I said. "What's a sour ball?" Fleet described them as salty, bitter dried plums that had been dyed a bright red color. "The color resembles nothing in nature," he said. I told him I would go to the Viet Wah grocery that evening and see what I could find.

"That's the sort of place you want," he said. "Don't go to Uwajimaya, where you'll pay four times as much."

Over the weekend, Fred Wirth came back into the hospital for a tune-up. He had finally been committed to a nursing home after being scrubbed down and treated for lice. While at the nursing home he received six weeks of antibiotics to cure the bone infection, and his gangrenous toe finally sloughed off on its own, without surgery. The ulcers were healing nicely and the maggots were gone. When I visited with him the morning after his admission, Wirth smiled cheerfully and even seemed to remember me. "I feel great," he said, and asked whether he really had to stay in the hospital.

I promised to discharge him just as soon as the wound-care team gave their blessing, and then I moved on to the day's other discharges, which included the commercial diver—who was going home to Ballard with a right-arm cast, a left-leg cast, a single crutch, and an ex-wife to help him. *Surgical patients could be such a cinch to discharge*, I thought, *because they had homes, families, and because they were actually going to get better*. Geoff Morgan wanted to go home too, and because the fever was gone and his immune system had partway recovered, I decided he could go. I didn't know if I'd ever see him again.

"Kid, it's been real," he said.

My next stop was to see Kermit, who carefully studied the package of dried plums that I had brought him. The plums were individually wrapped, and he handed them back to me. "Get your money back," he insisted. ("Too elegant," Fleet would tell me later.) But Kermit tore into the package of red ginger, and as he bit into the first piece, a look of bliss crossed his face. By the time I was out the door and pointed toward Bert Burphy's room next door, Kermit's fingers had turned fiery red with the ginger stain.

Burphy told me that he had just heard he would be transferring to a rehabilitation facility early the next week, and then he started talking about paintings he'd inherited from his father, two of which were early Andrew Wyeth paintings.

"Signed, papers, all that," he said. He thought they were worth thirty grand apiece but he'd never looked into it. His dad could have sold them, but instead he'd passed them on for an unforeseen situation like this one, Burphy thought, where he might need the money. He continued to describe the pieces, and I wondered how I would work in my questions about his appetite and breathing, when he asked if I was interested in buying either of the paintings. I told him I was not going to take any family heirlooms from him under the circumstances, and I reminded him that Medicaid would be picking up his entire tab anyway, retroactive to the beginning of his injury, because his illness had been so severe and protracted.

"I'll believe it when I see it," he said. He was a middle-class guy with a home and a job, but he wasn't so rich that he could afford to be sentimental.

A few minutes later, I sat down to work on Burphy's summary, to guide the hospital doctor who was coming on the following week. It would take me an hour to review the hundred-some chart notes from the patient's hospitalization and type a record of his visit. As I clicked through the chart and wished I had the cash to buy original art, I thought of how a story that began with a broken leg could end as a story about liquidating the family assets. The guy had been cleaning his gutters. It could happen to anyone.

A Vision

One summer morning, Scott Barnhart paged to tell me that the hospital had fifty-five boarders, and said, laughing, that he was putting all of them on my service.

"Seriously, we're very full. Whatever you can do to get people out would be great." The PA system announced the census status as Code Brown, a designation with which I was not familiar.

The news came that Geoff Morgan had passed away peacefully at home. His memorial service took place in a sprawling suburban church decorated with enormous bouquets of blue and yellow lilies. There were recountings of his eBay odysseys and his best practical jokes, and Nanette was lovely and gracious. At the reception afterward she told me how grateful she was for the extra time with him.

Bert Burphy emailed to say that the metal cage around his shattered leg had finally been removed and he was starting to get around with a cane. He was soon to marry the most fantastic woman he had ever known, he said.

Kermit Jackson escaped from his latest nursing home not long after discharge—he had a prognosis of just a few days to live—and some hours later he rolled into the ED, complaining of mistreatment at his new home. The problem?

He wanted his wardrobe dry-cleaned before he died. His funeral took place at the fringe of a gentrifying neighborhood, in a white-and-pink stucco church that was packed with hundreds of people, some clutching elaborate hats in their laps and waving a free hand in the air. A cousin came to the pulpit and said, "We now bring you an unconventional service for an unconventional brother."

A nephew leapt up and began to play Kermit's favorite song, a Stevie Wonder number. His mourners rose, clapping and dancing and shouting, and for a moment I wondered whether Kermit might rise from his casket, a shiny white affair strewn with red carnations, make his way up to the stage, and start playing the horn he loved so much. He had always seemed so much larger than the illnesses that had laid claim to his body over the years. But he was really gone now, and for me his death marked another ending of sorts. Kermit was the last of my patients to survive from my first days at the hospital, when the story of Harborview was, for me, a much simpler story about caring for the poor.

It wasn't until I was deep into writing this book that I recognized Harborview's story as that of a successful business. The evidence was compelling: in my five years there, the hospital's charity care efforts had tripled, to $112 million per year on $550 million of revenue, and yet the organization continued to run in the black despite limited government support. Today Harborview is as well positioned to survive turbulent times as any safety net hospital can be, and the credit lies with the management and their long-term business plan.

Of course, the business plan doesn't always translate into clinical practice as smoothly as one might hope. Even when the hospital is full to the gills, the administration protects beds for patients requiring complex surgical procedures. The private rooms on Six remain private, and it's no pleasure watching selected patients wait for transfer elsewhere during a space crunch. The fact is that Harborview is one of a very few places in our society with no comfortable distance between the truly wealthy and the desperately poor, where there are no buffers like separate neighborhoods and separate schools to anesthetize against the sting of disparity.

With time, I've come to believe that Harborview is a much stronger institution because of its business orientation, its need to attract paying patients. Had there been a more vigorous stream of government money, the hospital may never have undergone such intense efforts to improve the quality of medical care and to cut waste, or to develop its specialty franchises that bring in well-heeled clients. Under duress, the administration has managed to build a financial engine for the hospital, and the hospital's ability to care for people from "all walks of life" has proven sustaining, especially as charity care demands grow.

It's enough to make one wonder whether massive government outlays to safety-net hospitals do little more than maintain the status quo, little more than forestall the system's complete collapse. This is not to say that we can solve our health care problems simply by slashing public funding. What we should pay attention to is Harborview's novel operational model, its practice of directing "profits" into health care for all, rather than to stockholders or whoever else is occupying the organizational pinnacle. The Harborview model works because all of the staff make sacrifices, including those at the executive and professional levels, and because everybody is working toward something larger than their own financial gain.

Harborview's story also provides a telling window into our health care system. The hospital will increase surgical capacity by 50 percent and raise critical care capabilities significantly, because these services pay handsomely, and not necessarily because they serve the broader public best. While Scott Barnhart and I were talking one afternoon, he suggested that I consult the *Dartmouth Atlas of Health Care*, an extensive body of research showing that systems focused on specialty care are ultimately more expensive and often produce worse health outcomes than systems with a strong primary care focus. But what can Harborview do with this information? The hospital won't expand primary care services as long as they are losing money, and these services are likely to lose money for as long as the market continues to undervalue primary care.

In fact, the health care market is interested primarily in treating disease, the more complex the better, and the reimbursement system reflects our sense that treatments and cures are what make for great health care. Clearly, there are occasions in which technological innovations work miracles, but there are also so many instances in which we simply acquiesce to the over-medicalization of our lives, instances in which medical treatment does little to relieve the anguish of disease, aging or death, let alone improve health. We dialyze people who are dead, as Fleet says. Enormous sums are spilled in the last six months of a person's life. How can it make sense to withhold our spending until there's little left to gain, and then blow it all?

But we are nowhere near a rational dialogue about how we might begin to limit medical care—that would smack too much of *socialism*—and so we permit unchecked growth and out-of-control health care costs. We spend more than double what any other country does for health care, and for our generosity, we rank near the bottom of the heap in the most health basic measures, like life expectancy. This seeming paradox unravels only when viewed in light of the 20 percent of Americans without reliable health insurance, many of whom can only access medical care in emergency departments.

Our present health care system represents universal medical care at rock bottom. It is a system that forces certain individuals to delay medical attention until a problem has reached crisis proportions, a system that provides, for these patients, the most acute and superficial solutions at some of the steepest prices in the world. The costs of caring for these individuals are generally so high that the rest of us end up footing the bill; in 2005, $922 of an average family's health insurance premium went to cover the uninsured— and that doesn't factor in the $600 billion we paid toward Medicare and Medicaid. Despite the enormous sums being spent, though, we have little to show in the way of new-found health for these individuals, who generally cannot afford the follow-up care and medications they commonly require, and who continue to have great difficulty finding providers to see them on an ongoing basis.

We cannot solve our health care crisis without specifically addressing how we care for the uninsured. Central to the matter is that poor and uninsured patients often suffer from greater stress and more advanced illness than everyone else. We don't really know how best to take care of these individuals—more doctors and nurses? home visits? cooking and nutrition classes? And maybe the better solutions are structural ones, like improved education and job opportunities, but nobody knows for sure. For so long, the medical community has competed *not* to care for the poor, rather than competing to provide better care, as we do for those with ample resources. No one should be surprised that we have so few solutions for this population.

There is a lot of catch-up work to do. I believe that experimentation and innovation are our best hope, and it seems likely that the solutions we settle on won't look anything like those currently under scrutiny. The example of Seattle's experimental wet house shows just how challenging it can be to see beyond the status quo, to do something as revolutionary as meeting people where they are, rather than where we believe they should be. Instead we lean heavily on our moral sensibilities, on our myths about poverty, and not enough on scientific proof about what can really help. Experimentation may be our salvation. If we're picking up the tab anyway, perhaps it makes more sense to house a human being than to pay for ever-recurring ED visits. Perhaps it's a fair exchange if the wet house offloads the courts and increases capacity in the jail and county detox facility.

Probably the single thing with the greatest power to stabilize our nation's health in this day and age is universal health insurance coverage. The timing could not be any more critical. As the U.S. economy slides into a prolonged recession and our best businesses fight for their lives, we each face the very real prospect of losing health care coverage and never regaining it again. For many individuals, the loss of health insurance is increasingly accompanied by mounting medical debt, which can delay or preclude activities like completing an advanced degree, engaging in career retraining, or starting a new business—in other words, the very activities that nourish societies during hard times.

Designing a functional and appealing system will take considerable work, though. We must remain open to many possible solutions, since our initial reforms are likely to have major flaws—*and* be very expensive. We must take a hard look at what it means to be poor or uninsured and reconsider our misty ideas about what's fair, about self-reliance and rising up by the bootstraps. We must seek out and reward hybrid organizations that work toward all of our purposes. And we must be prepared to face powerful political forces, like the pharmaceutical and insurance lobbyists, and the professional physician organizations that are forever twisting health care into new vehicles to serve their own needs.

As doctors are known to say, this will not be painless. Experimentation with universal systems of coverage has begun at the state level, in Oregon, Hawaii, Maine, and Massachusetts; already these systems have brought on the uncontrolled growth in health care costs that goes along with previously underinsured individuals accessing necessary services. But we should be glad that these programs will teach us what works and what doesn't, and hopefully we'll withhold our judgment long enough to glean some wisdom from these grand experiments.

In tough times, we behave as though we are all in this together, and this may be the most enduring lesson of Harborview's story, whose heroes are as much the rank-and-file staff and hospital executives as they are outsized personalities like Dr. Fleet and Dr. Copass. I have come to understand that justice is not the sacred province of nurses and doctors and social workers. Human wholeness is shared work, and health justice demands a broad coalition of actors. Health justice depends on activists and attorneys, on entrepreneurs, computer programmers, schoolteachers, financiers, taxi drivers, and above all, on the seemingly ordinary citizens who decide to challenge the status quo, who decide it is high time to take up the fight. Justice, in the end, must come from human inspiration. At stake is nothing less than our collective health.

Appendix A: Learn More

Life Support

Two excellent resources on the historical role of hospitals are Charles Rosenberg's *The Care of Strangers: the Rise of America's Hospital System* (The Johns Hopkins University Press, 1987) and Rosemary Stevens's *In Sickness and In Wealth: American Hospitals in the Twentieth Century* (The Johns Hopkins University Press, 1989). Rosenberg tells the history of hospitals through the early twentieth century, and Stevens focuses on hospital developments in the twentieth century.

The impact of American physician professional organizations on our present health care system is brilliantly documented in Paul Starr's Pulitzer Prize–winning *The Social Transformation of American Medicine* (Basic Books, 1982).

Jan de Hartog's 1964 novel, *The Hospital,* was an exposé of the wretched conditions at Houston's Jefferson Davis charity hospital, which may not have been too different from conditions in other urban public hospitals.

Detailed information about public hospitals is available in "America's Public Hospitals and Health Systems, 2004," a report by Obaid Zaman, Ellen Lukens, and Linda Cummings, published in 2006 by the National Association of Public Hospitals (NAPH), Washington D.C., and online at www.naph.org.

Sequel

About 16 percent of Americans have no health insurance, including 27.3 million working adults, and many millions only have intermittent coverage, as detailed in "Income, Poverty, and Health Insurance Coverage in the United States: 2005," published by the U.S. Census Bureau. Patients without insurance receive fewer preventive services and are more likely to delay needed medical care, in Diamant, A.L. et al, "Delays and Unmet Need for Health Care Among Adult Primary Care Patients in a Restructured Urban Public Health System," *American Journal of Public Health* 2004; vol. 94, pgs. 783–89, and Sudano, J.J. and Baker, D.W., "Intermittent Lack of Health Insurance Coverage and Use of Preventive Services," *American Journal of Public Health* 2003; vol. 93: pgs. 130–37.

Appendix A

We provide de facto universal health care through our emergency rooms, thanks to a 1986 law called the Emergency Medical Treatment and Labor Act (EMTALA), which was intended to protect access to emergency medical services regardless of a patient's ability to pay. As a result of this law, and the absence of any other mandate to provide health care to all, EDs have become the first point of contact in the health care system for many of the uninsured, and EDs are now often overloaded with these patients. It has become clear that the ED is a very expensive and inefficient setting in which to treat the tens of millions of people who need access to routine medical care; the thinking in the ED generally focuses on solving only the patient's immediate problems. See Jonathan Glauser's "Rationing and the Role of the Emergency Department as Society's Safety Net," *Academic Emergency Medicine*, November 2001, vol. 8, pgs. 1101–6.

The cost of caring for the uninsured is picked up by everyone else. Based on data compiled from several government databases, including the U.S. Census, health services researcher Kenneth E. Thorpe of Emory University and the advocacy organization Families USA estimate that $922 of the typical family health insurance premium in 2005 went to cover the cost of the uninsured (the average family paid $226 per month for health insurance that year). This cost is expected to rise to $1,502 per family by 2010. One-twelfth of health insurance fees paid by employers goes to fund care for the uninsured.

Even though the poor and uninsured may not pay the full cost of their care, hospital bills can still hit hard, and some hospitals have pursued aggressive collections practices. See "Uncharitable?" by Jonathan Cohn, in *The New York Times*, December 19, 2004. Cohn's book, *Sick: The Untold Story of America's Health Care Crisis—and the People Who Pay the Price* (HarperCollins, 2007), documents the dramatic consequences that befall individuals without health insurance, and presents his argument for a single-payer health care system.

An intriguing argument about health inequality comes from Stephen Bezruchka, an emergency physician and epidemiologist at the University of Washington, who argues that inadequate nutrition, medical care, education, etc. do not fully account for health inequities, and that poverty itself can cause illness. See "Hierarchy and Health are Related" in *British Medical Journal*, vol. 324, pg. 978 and "The Status Syndrome:

How Social Standing Affects Our Health and Longevity" in *The New England Journal of Medicine*, vol. 352, pgs. 1159–60.

Frequent Flyers
The joint operating agreement between the University of Washington, which manages Harborview's daily operations, and the King County government, which provides capital for building projects, was established in 1967 and has been updated periodically, most recently on July 1, 1995.

Diversion
Pharmaceutical industry strategies are described in numerous recent works including *The Truth About the Drug Companies: How They Deceive Us and What to Do About It* (Random House, 2004) by former *New England Journal of Medicine* editor Marcia Angell. More recent is Howard Brody's *Hooked: How Medicine's Dependence on the Pharmaceutical Industry Undermines Professional Ethics* (Rowman & Littlefield, 2007).

David Blumenthal reviewed the scientific evidence on pharmaceutical industry interactions with physicians in "Doctors and Drug Companies," *New England Journal of Medicine* 2004, vol. 351, pgs. 1885–90.

Black Friday
A brief on our national preparedness for disasters: "Hospital Staffing and Surge Capacity During a Disaster Event," published by NAPH, Washington D.C., May 2007.

Under Construction
Many public hospitals have closed in recent years, and the hostile environment for these organizations is described in the Institute of Medicine report, *America's Health Care Safety Net: Intact but Endangered*, (National Academy Press, 2000). Also see Dennis P. Andrulis and Lisa M. Duchon's report, "Hospital Care in the 100 Largest Cities and Their Suburbs, 1996–2002: Implications for the Future of the Hospital Safety Net in Metropolitan America," August 2005, published by SUNY Downstate Medical Center.

Joel Weissman's "The Trouble with Uncompensated Hospital Care," in *The New England Journal of Medicine* 2005; vol. 352: pgs. 1171–73, describes the challenge of hospitals' acting charitably while also still functioning competitively.

The classic for-profit and not-for-profit organizational models may have limited utility in health care, particularly for public hospitals, as Bruce Siegel concluded in a 1996 report procuced for the Commonwealth Fund, "Public Hospitals—A Prescription for Survival." Business professor R. Edward Freeman has advocated for a philosophy that he calls "Stakeholder Theory," under which corporations address the needs of all of its stakeholders, not just its financial shareholders; see "Business Ethics and Health Care: A Stakeholder Perspective," *Health Care Management Review* 2002; vol. 27: pgs. 52–65; Mattia J. Gilmartin is the lead author on this paper. Along these lines, one of the more intriguing books to come out recently about health care reform comes from Michael E. Porter and Elizabeth Olmsted Teisberg, *Redefining Health Care: Creating Value-Based Competition on Results* (Harvard Business School Publishing, 2006).

Denver General Hospital has been highly innovative in its care of the medically underserved. "Hospitals Try Free Basic Care for Uninsured," by Eric Eckholm, *The New York Times*, October 25, 2006. The article describes the plans of Denver General and other hospitals around the county to provide primary care services for all patients, in hopes to decreasing advanced illness and thus the need for expensive care. Also see: Patricia Gabow and colleagues' "Denver Health: a Model for the Integration of a Public Hospital and Community Health Centers," in *Annals of Internal Medicine* 2003; vol. 138: pgs. 143–49.

Bunks for Drunks

Early data shows that the Housing First approach may be the most effective option for patients with substance abuse and mental illness. See "Housing First, Consumer Choice, and Harm Reduction for Homeless Individuals with a Dual Diagnosis" by Sam Tsemberis, Leyla Gulcur, and Maria Nakae, *American Journal of Public Health* 2004; vol. 94: pgs. 651–56.

Scott Barnhart and Bill Block argue cogently against the passive approach to homelessness in "We Have to Do More Than Maintain the Homeless Problem," *Seattle Post-Intelligencer*, November 22, 2006.

A Vision

Many people in the health policy, health services, and business sectors have written about the need for systemic change in health care.

One desperately needed system upgrade must come in how we provide health care to the poor and uninsured, who get sicker and more expensive all the time. However, we know very little about caring for these vulnerable populations. Miranda Tsai and colleagues have documented one example of this in "Identifying Homelessness at an Urban Public Hospital: a Moving Target?" in *Journal of Health Care for the Poor and Underserved* 2005; vol. 16: pgs. 297–307.

In any case, potential solutions for health system overhaul abound. Clayton Christensen has published extensively about disruptive innovations, which are new services and products aimed at previously unrecognized markets. When disruptive innovations are adopted widely, as with Southwest Airlines' low-cost airplane tickets, they can change not only how who the customers are but how customers are spending money. In "Disruptive Innovation for Social Change," *Harvard Business Review*, December 2006, pgs. 94–101, Christensen et al argue that disruptive innovations can bring simpler, more affordable health care products and services to a broad population. Also see "Disruptive Innovation: Can Health Care Learn from Other Industries? A Conversation with Clayton M. Christensen," by Mark D. Smith in *Health Affairs 2007*, pgs. w288–w295, and Christensen's *Innovator's Prescription: A Disruptive Solution for Health Care* (McGraw-Hill, 2008).

Richard A. Deyo and Donald L. Patrick write about our obsession with new technology and our rush to adopt these products without real proof of their efficacy in *Hope or Hype: the Obsession with Medical Advances and the High Cost of False Promises*, (AMACOM/American Management Association, 2005). Many health policy experts believe that this focus on medical technology and specialization have raised the cost of health care dramatically *and* worsened health outcomes. In "Medical Care—Is More Always Better?" from *The New England Journal of Medicine* 2003, vol. 349, pgs. 1665–67, Elliot Fisher argues that more medical care is not necessarily better, and in the U.S. is associated with worse health outcomes. He and his colleagues in health outcomes research at Dartmouth, including the notorious John E. Wennberg, have convincingly demonstrated that medical practices are influenced by regional factors as much as anything else: see Wennberg, Fisher, and Skinner, "Geography and the Debate Over Medicare Reform," *Health Affairs 2002*; pgs. w96–w114.

Appendix A

Health services researcher Kenneth E. Thorpe has found that nearly two-thirds of the increase in health care spending is due to increasing disease prevalence (meaning we are spending our money on potentially preventable conditions like diabetes, obesity, and heart disease), new technologies, and new patterns in diagnosis and treatment (we now prescribe medication for asymptomatic diseases). Health promotion may save money, he writes, but little research has been done on interventions. See "The Rise in Health Care Spending and What to Do About It." *Health Affairs 2005*; vol. 24, pgs. 1436–45.

The economist David M. Cutler suggests that as medical care costs rise, so does the value we extract from it, in *Your Money or Your Life: Strong Medicine for America's Health Care System*. (Oxford University Press, 2005).

Change comes bit by bit to most health care systems and not in one massive sweep, as Atul Gawande describes in "Getting From There to Here" in *The New Yorker* (January 26, 2009).

Appendix B: How to Help

1. **Donate money.** As one Harborview administrator said, money is the lifeblood of any organization. Learn about service organizations in your area that are implementing novel solutions to long-standing problems. The Downtown Emergency Service Center (DESC) in Seattle is one such organization that provides housing for individuals who suffer from substance abuse or mental illness, which helps to stabilize lives: 515 Third Avenue, Seattle, WA 98104; (206) 464-1570; www.desc.org.

2. **Support health care systems that provide equitable, high-quality care.** Hospitals are required to disclose the level of charity care and community service they provide. Sometimes the numbers tell a different story than the public relations office.

3. **Get informed.** Read books and newspapers and stay abreast of the issues. Even better, witness soup kitchens, jails, free clinics, crisis counseling centers, and shelters firsthand.

4. **Get involved.** Commit to helping an underserved individual or group, or to advocating for an issue important to you over an extended period of time. Making a difference requires sustained effort. A couple of weekends of volunteer work will get you inspired and feeling good, but real change requires commitment.

5. **Tell your legislators how you feel.** Grassroots movements can really have an impact on which bills are passed. Input from constituents can be very effective, in spite of what we hear about high-profile lobbying efforts.

Notes and Acknowledgments

Dozens of people contributed to the making of this book. I owe my deepest debt of gratitude to the patients in these stories, who appear under altered names and identities.

Several of my colleagues and mentors were particularly generous with their time and energy, and their contributions are reflected throughout the book: Alice Brownstein, Sam Warren, Anneliese Schleyer, Scott Barnhart, Michael Copass, and Patrick Fleet. It is a high privilege to have worked with you.

I'd like to note here that for purposes of narrative simplification, Alice Brownstein represented the role of the entire ED junta, which also includes Sam Warren, David Baker, David Carlbom, and Bob Kalus. Each of these individuals had helpful input.

Those who helped me to understand how the hospital operates included Marv Turck, Sig Hansen, Johnese Spisso, Pamela Harrell, Ken Jarman, Lucy Berliner, Ellie Graham, Peter Lee, Susan Gregg-Hanson, and Pamela Steele. Bill Hobson, Executive Director of DESC, provided valuable background information about Seattle's shelter system.

I received helpful commentary on the manuscript from Caroline Rhoads, Hillary Liss, Justin Goodman, Jake Bartholomy, Yung Lie, Vicki Mau, and Nassim Assefi. Special thanks to Sherri Schultz and Jane Huntington for editorial input, and to John Coulter for his advocacy.

I'd like to thank the staff at Sasquatch: specifically Gary Luke and Rachelle Longé, as well as my agent Max Gartenberg, who worked patiently with me until the book was right.

And thank you to my husband, Charlie Crissman, who does more than I can acknowledge here.

This book is for those who dedicate their lives to the Harborview mission, especially Erin Reed, Lois Suzuki, and Steve Smith.

About the Author

Audrey Young, MD, was most recently Assistant Professor of Medicine at the University of Washington in Seattle and a staff physician at Seattle's county hospital, Harborview Medical Center. She holds a BA in history from UC Berkeley. She is the author of *What Patients Taught Me* (Sasquatch Books, 2004) and has been called a "fine storyteller" by *People* magazine. She and her husband live in Seattle.